STREET NAMES
of the
CITY OF GLASGOW

— A New Historical Guide —

For Mum & John

Street Names
of the
City of Glasgow
— A New Historical Guide —

CAROL FOREMAN

JOHN DONALD PUBLISHERS LTD
EDINBURGH

ISBN 0 85976 482 6

British Library Cataloguing in Publication Data.
A catalogue record for this book is available
from the British Library.

Typesetting and PostScript origination by Brinnoven, Livingston.
Printed & bound in Great Britain by Bell & Bain Ltd, Glasgow.

PREFACE

Most people have thought at one time or another 'I wonder how that street got its name?', myself included. On trying to research the subject *vis-a-vis* Glasgow's streets I discovered nothing had been written about them since 1901. I decided to set this oversight to rights and began compiling *Street Names of the City of Glasgow* which explains the origins and history of some of the city's street names. I say *some*, as it's impossible within the limits of a single volume to detail them all. What I did was to choose an area to work within, concentrating particularly on the city centre — to the north, the M8, to the south, the north bank of the River Clyde, east to Glasgow Green and Bridgeton, and west to the Kingston Bridge.

This book is neither a street directory nor an architectural guide, although particular buildings of note have been included. Some streets have been missed out, their names being self-explanatory, and some because they were named after worthy but uninteresting people. Others were culled for reasons of space and some defied my powers of research. I simply couldn't find out how they got their names. Many are nothing more than signposts today, but have been included because their names are so quaint and tied up with the ancient history of Glasgow that they should not be lost in the mists of time. I hope you will be forgiving if your favourite street has been omitted.

Streets derive their names from a variety of sources that often indicate the date they were laid out — local associations, sentiment, distinguished persons, historical events, etc.

During my research I wore out much shoe leather tramping round Glasgow and all the information about the condition of buildings or the existence of streets was, to the best of my knowledge, correct at the time of publication. However, in a city things change all the time. Buildings that have lain derelict for years are restored to their former glory; others are demolished.

New streets appear; old ones vanish. I would also like to explain that some buildings no longer have their original numbers. Therefore when I mention that a certain establishment was at No. x in a particular street a century ago, although the building still stands it may have a different address today.

As a number of the street names have conflicting explanations as to their origin, it's possible many of you will be aware of some which differ from those given. If so, I would not be averse to hearing what they are. Also, if any glaring errors have been made, please excuse them, as I didn't intend to write a mini-history of Glasgow when I started the book. However, the more I delved into the past and fact after fact on every aspect of the city came to light, that's how it developed. After all, it's people and events that make a street, not impersonal buildings.

C.F.
1997

CONTENTS

ORDER AND ABBREVIATIONS

For speedy reference, street names have been arranged in alphabetical order (see also p. vii). To facilitate location, main headings in the text are accompanied by the appropriate (abbreviated) district name in brackets as follows:

(B/law)	Broomielaw
(c/c)	City Centre
(C/caddens)	Cowcaddens
(C/dral)	Cathedral
(comm/c)	Commercial Centre
(C/ton)	Calton
(e/g/g)	East Glasgow Green
(g/g)	Glasgow Green
(G/gate)	Gallowgate
(G/hill)	Garnethill
(m/c)	Merchant City
(N/lis)	Necropolis
(St/E)	St Enoch
(S/mkt)	Saltmarket
(T/head)	Townhead

Note

Glasgow grew in two parts. The religious centre around the Cathedral and the salmon fishing village beside the River Clyde. Gradually High Street linked the two communities, and eight streets evolved — High Street, Rottenrow, Drygate, Trongate, Gallowgate, Saltmarket, Stockwell and Bridgegate. By 1750 Bell Street, Candleriggs, Canon Street, King Street and Princes Street (Now Parnie Street) had been added, bringing the total to thirteen.

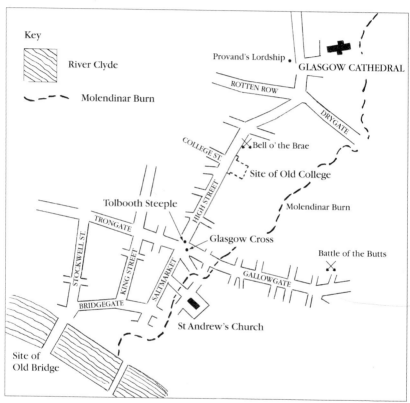

Key

River Clyde

Molendinar Burn

Provand's Lordship

GLASGOW CATHEDRAL

ROTTEN ROW

DRYGATE

COLLEGE ST.

Bell o' the Brae

Site of Old College

Molendinar Burn

HIGH STREET

Tolbooth Steeple

TRONGATE

STOCKWELL ST.

KING STREET

SALTMARKET

Glasgow Cross

Battle of the Butts

GALLOWGATE

BRIDGEGATE

St Andrew's Church

Site of
Old Bridge

Rough Map. Streets of Old Glasgow.

STREET NAMES OF THE CITY OF GLASGOW

Abercromby Street (C/ton)

In early times the road east from the city ran from the Drygate to Ladywell Street, over the Gallowmuir, along the Witch Loan to Barrowfield and the Dalmarnock Ford where the Clyde was crossed. Old maps clearly show Witch Loan (said to have been created by the masons who built the cathedral and lived in Rutherglen) part of which was north and part south of Gallowgate. The southern part was named Abercromby Street (1802) in

Sir Raplh Abercromby

honour of Sir Ralph Abercromby, a distinguished British General mortally wounded at Aboukir during the Battle of the Nile in the war for Egypt against Napoleon. Extreme shortsightedness contributed to his recklessness in battle, eventually costing him his life. The section of Abercromby Street which meets London Road was originally called Clyde Street, after local brewer John Clyde.

The northern part of Witch Loan became Bellgrove, 'Bel' signifying a prominence, or 'belle' for beautiful. Bellgrove was once a narrow road with a row of trees down each side and a small ditch running from Duke Street to Gallowgate. On the east, at the top, stood Annfield Park, containing Annfield House said to be haunted by a white lady, and, on the west, villas with gardens where some married officers lived with their families when the infantry was in Gallowgate Barracks. Recognised as the centre of the district, on holiday evenings such as Queen Victoria's birthday, Bellgrove Street was crowded.

Albion Street (c/c)

Albion is one of the ancient Gaelic names for Scotland. Built on church lands, the street opened around 1808. From the earliest July Town Council minute existing, that of 1574, it appears to have been the practice to hold a ritualistic open-court of the Burgh on 'Fair-even', 6 July. This took place on a piece of rocky ground called Craignacht, somewhere in the region of today's North Albion Street, the fair itself being held in the garden of the adjoining Greyfriars Monastery. In 1820, Greyfriars United Seccession Church was built on the site of the old Monastery from which it took its name. Demolished in 1972, a car park replaced it.

Along Albion Street's west side, just north of Ingram Street, is the mainly glass and black vitrolite former *Daily Express* Building (1936) now occupied by *The Herald* and *Evening Times*.

Anderston

John Anderston, owner of Stobcross Estate, the land on which it was built, named it after himself 'Anderston's Town' which became better known as Anderston. Around 1725 he decided to feu a village on an unprofitable section of his land near Gushet Farm, later Anderston Cross, now part of the Kingston Bridge. Only a few mean thatched dwellings were built, and it was not until John Orr of Barrowfield bought the estate in 1735 that the hamlet enlarged. Weavers took up the first feus and some street names derived from their processes — Carding Lane, Loom Place, Warp Lane — all sadly gone. Industries were established — 1751 Delftfield Potteries, 1762 Anderston Brewing Company and 1776 the famous Verreville Glassworks with its distinctive cone shaped chimney.

Anderston Main Street. These houses, built around 1780, were on the south side of the Main Street. Much of Anderston disappeared in the 1970s in the wake of Glasgow's ringroad.

Anderston's Coat-of-Arms

Anderston became a Burgh on 24 June 1824, a privilege it only enjoyed for 22 years before being annexed in 1846 by its big brother, Glasgow. As its coat-of-arms, the Burgh adopted that of the Anderstons of Stobcross with a few additions. A leopard with a spool in its mouth, a craftsman and a merchant symbolising trade and commerce and a ship in full sail representing foreign trade. Its motto: 'The one flourishes by the help of the other'.

Argyle Street (c/c)

Nearly two miles long, Argyle Street is split into two contrasting parts. From Trongate to the magnificent Central Station viaduct it's bright and cheerful and one of Scotland's busiest streets (Glaswegians describe any place packed to the gunnels as being 'like Argyle Street on a Saturday') and beyond that drab and uninspiring.

As late as 1750 what is now Argyle Street was entirely out of town, the city's western boundary being the West Port Gate at the head of Stockwell. Immediately outside this was an unpaved rural road — which over the years went by the names of St Enoch's Gait, Dumbarton Road, and Westergait (the way to the west) — with a few malt kilns or barns and a handful of one-storey thatched houses. The last of these old buildings, a thatched malt kiln at the corner of Argyle/Mitchell Streets, was demolished about 1830.

After the Council took down the West Port Gate and Provosts Murdoch and Dunlop built twin mansions in 1750 the street rapidly filled, becoming Argyle Street around 1761 in honour of Archibald, 3rd Duke of Argyll (spelling was flexible then). A short time later he was dead. His funeral cortège passed through Glasgow on its way to the family burial grounds at Kilmun and ironically, his body lay in the city's most fashionable hostelry, the Black Bull Inn in the very street so recently named after him. Marks & Spencer's store occupies the site of the Black Bull which Robert Burns visited in 1787/88, an association commemorated by a plaque on the store's Virginia Street wall.

Across from Marks is the site of Grafton's Ladies Fashion Store, the scene of a tragic fire in 1949 when 13 women and girls

Dunlop Mansion in 1889 when it had come down in the world by being converted into shops.

died. Five employees were saved by climbing along the building's top storey ledge, crossing the roof of the adjoining Argyle Cinema, and then dropping a considerable distance to the next building's roof (the old Dunlop mansion) where firemen with ladders rescued them. Others jumped into Argyle Street where thousands of passers-by gathered to watch the spectacle.

John Anderson's Royal Polytechnic (the 'Poly' to all), took up the whole block between Dunlop Street and Maxwell Street. He introduced the department store to Scotland in the 1840s and claimed to have pioneered the idea of universal trading under one roof, his philosophy being 'keen prices for a quick return'. In 1925 his son sold out to Lewis's who gradually rebuilt the old Poly into the largest provincial department store in the country. The interior was modernised in 1988 and Debenhams now occupy the building.

Diagonally across from Debenhams to the west is Scotland's oldest covered walkway, the Argyll Arcade (1828) built by John Robertson Reid, who toured Europe studying arcades before deciding what to give Glasgow. He and architect John Baird came

Thatched Malt Kiln at corner of Mitchell/Argyle Streets drawn about 1820.

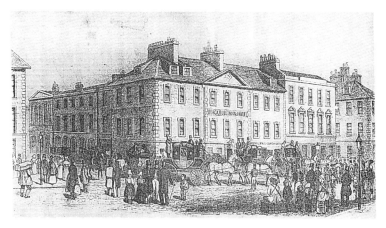

Black Bull Coaching Inn, the site now occupied by Marks & Spencer.

Argyle Street in the 1920s.

up with an elegant, Parisian style, hammerbeamed, glass roofed structure which connected Argyle Street with Buchanan Street. From the beginning, children adored visiting the Arcade loving the sheer magic of what appeared to them to be a 'brightly-lit cave' and the excitement of entering from one street and coming out in another.

Just west of the arcade is Cranston House (the former Crown Tea Rooms), an 18th-century building gifted to Kate Cranston by her bridegroom in 1892 which she had remodelled with projecting eaves, gables, fancy dormers and tower with spire. The interior was by George Walton and the furnishings by Charles Rennie Mackintosh, who, in 1907, turned the basement into a Dutch Kitchen with a fireplace as its focal point. A recent renovation uncovered the fireplace and decorative tiles which were photographed for posterity.

Directly across the road from Cranston House is the neat twin towered building that survived a demolition order in 1935. It opened in Edwardian days as Crouch's Palace of Varieties, became the Wonderland Theatre, then the St Enoch Picture Theatre, and today Dolcis and Evans occupy it.

The massive domed warehouse (1903) built at the north west corner of Argyle/Buchanan Streets for Stewart & Macdonald Ltd has two giant sculptured figures supporting the Argyle Street doorway which were cheekily nicknamed 'Stewart' and 'Macdonald' after the proprietors.

West of the Central Station viaduct to the motorway about all of interest is the Blythswood Hotel and the Clydesdale Bank. Definitely not of interest is the giant, concrete white elephant, the Anderston Centre (1972).

The first mention of Argyle Street in a business sense was in 1783 when R Browne, Perfumer, advertised that he supplied 'genuine violet powder for the hair of a neat, elegant and cheerful kind'. Around 1828, plumber George Douglas installed the city's first plate glass windows in shops he owned on the north side of Argyle Street just east of Buchanan Street. It was considered generally 'a great risk and monstrous extravagance'. In 1891 at No. 42, pool could be played every evening for one shilling an hour at the Union Billiard Rooms, the largest in Scotland.

Bain Street/Square (C/ton)

In the heart of Barrowland, this area was driven through the narrow closes of New Street (including the notorious 'Whisky Close') as part of the City Improvement Trust's programme to get rid of the town's worst slums. It was named after James Bain (Provost 1873–77) whose wealth of knowledge and business experience proved to be of great service to the Council.

Flanking an entrance to the Barrows in Bain Street is the former William White Clay Pipe Factory (1877) which, in its heyday, produced around 14,400 pipes per day in 700 designs. The distinctive red-yellow brick façade was originally intended to be stone, but costs determined otherwise.

Barrack Street (G/gate)

Built on lands anciently known as the Butts where the Burghers mustered at the Wappenschaw (weapon-showing) to practise Archery, hence the Butts. It was there in 1544 during the minority of Mary, Queen of Scots, that the bloody Battle of the Butts was

Sir James Bain.

Barrack Street 1885, drawn by David Small.

fought between Regent Arran and the Earl of Lennox. Although 300 fell on either side Arran won, and Glasgow, who supported Lennox, was plundered with even the windows and doors of the buildings being taken away. Covenanting times saw another battle in the same place. Defeated at the Battle of Drumclog in 1769, Claverhouse retreated to Glasgow. Encouraged by their success the Covenanters entered the city and clashed with royalist soldiers who ambushed them in the Gallowgate. This time they lost and Claverhouse gave orders not to bury his enemies' dead bodies, but to leave them to be eaten by the butchers' dogs.

A large portion of the land was gifted to the Government in 1795 as a site for infantry barracks and Barrack Street, opened the same year, was so named, as it formed the eastern boundary of the barracks which accommodated 1,000 men and cost £15,000. Previously soldiers were billeted on the inhabitants. The first regiment to occupy the quarters was the Argyllshire Fencibles, commanded by the Marquis of Lorne, later Duke of Argyll. When, a century later, new barracks were built in the north west of the city, the council hoped the War Office would hand the ground it had enjoyed the free use of back to the city for use as a much needed open garden space. But no, it was sold for a very large sum to a railway company.

There was a pighouse in Barrack Street — not a curing house for pork, but a pottery. 'Pig' was a Scottish term used for domestic earthenware said to derive from the Gaelic *pigadu,* an earthenware jug. Nowadays 'Pig' is confined to hot water bottles, but it used to refer to pottery chimney-cans and people used to say after a storm that 'a pig had fallen aff the lum'. The Water Authority dug up several misfits of these wares in 1913 and deposited them with the People's Palace.

Barras (Barrowland) (C/ton)

Most people believe that the name 'Barras', Glasgow's famous weekend street market, is a corruption of 'the barrows', but there are more likely explanations of the nickname. The old city Gallowgate Port was called 'The Eyst Barrasyet', which means gate in, or beside, a barrier. Alternatively, the ground occupied by the 'Barras' was part of the ancient Barrowfield lands, said to mean either 'the Burrow or Burgh Field'.

Regardless of the name's origin, there is no doubt as to how the market came about. Few hawkers owned their own barrows and in the early 1920s Maggie and James McIver were in the business of renting them out to stallholders around Gallowgate at one shilling and sixpence per week from their yard in Marshalls Lane. (Incidentally, it was in this lane that the first purpose built catholic chapel in Glasgow was constructed). When several tenements were demolished in the area, the McIvers bought the ground to use as a permanent market site. They built stalls, and by 1928 the market was roofed and enclosed. Maggie McIver became known as the 'Barrows Queen'.

The famous Barrowland Ballroom opened on Christmas Eve 1934. It was said that the building was one of those earmarked by Lord Haw-Haw as a target for the German Air Force during the Second World War. The reason — its popularity with the American Forces. Billy McGregor and his Barrowland Gaybirds were the resident band, but over the years many celebrity band-leaders appeared — Joe Loss, Henry Hall, Johnny Dankworth and Jack Hilton. Vocalists Lena Martell and Lulu both performed at Barrowland.

Bath Street (comm/c)

To commemorate the city's first public baths. In 1802, William Harley, a wealthy merchant, bought large stretches of the Blythswood Estate lands at Sauchie Haugh, where he built his house, Willowbank. To tempt people to build on his land he established a beautiful pleasure garden with summerhouse, bowling-green and thirty foot view-tower, known as Harley's Hill, or later Harley's Folly — where Blythswood Square now is.

When that novelty wore off he came up with another ambitious scheme. Supply water direct to the citizens' doors, all water then being available only from public wells. He purchased a long strip of land to the south of Sauchiehall Street and there built a roadway on the line of what is now Bath Street. From fine springs near his house he led water to a reservoir on Garnethill, and, using

William Harley.

special horse drawn four-wheeled carts ornamented on top with a gilt salmon, supplied the city with water at a halfpenny the stoup. Each King's Birthday, the carts, decorated with flowers, formed a procession. That was Glasgow's first effort to provide a public water supply on a large scale.

Taking advantage of the fad for 'taking the waters' he opened on his new road (at the corner of Bath/Renfield Streets) swimming and other baths with dressing rooms, reading rooms and various conveniences. Harley's road was nicknamed Bath Street which it remained.

Alongside the baths he built a byre for 24 cows to provide his customers with milk. Then it occurred to him that Glasgow was in need of a proper supply of pure sweet milk. The byre expanded to an immense dairy of over 200 cows, milk-houses and pigstyes. Everything was spotless and 'Harley's Byres' became a tourist attraction of Glasgow: even royalty visited them.

Alas, the Napoleonic Wars and speculative building developments ruined William Harley, and he died in 1829 *en route* to St

Petersburg to build a dairy for the Empress of Russia which may have restored his fortunes. Only the name of Bath Street remains to commemorate the enterprises of a man who was a true pioneer of the city.

Bath Street has three churches. Adelaide Place Baptist (1875), Elgin Place Congregational (1855) now a nightclub, and St Stephen's Renfield (1849) which has the street's only surviving steeple. At the bottom end of this still elegant street many original Georgian buildings remain, while, at the top end, Frank Matcham's red sandstone Kings Theatre (1904) and the Griffin Bar (originally Kings Arms 1903) with Art Nouveau woodwork and glass, are of particular interest.

Bell Street (m/c)

Some believe the first post-medieval street in the city (1710) was named after John Bell, a Lord Provost of Glasgow, but others are of the opinion it was after James Bell of Provosthaugh, who, among others, sold land and properties to the council in 1676 for the formation of a new street (Bell's Wynd). For this exercise, Provost Bell gets the honour.

An ardent royalist, he was present at the battle of Bothwell Bridge between covenanters and the Government's troops led by the Duke of Monmouth, an illegitimate son of King Charles II. After the fight he rode to Glasgow and in a few hours sent out all the bread he could find to the Royalist army and to each troop and company, a hogshead of wine taken from the cellars of those citizens who aided the rebels. John Bell's reward came on 27 October 1679. By warrant from Whitehall, the King authorised the Lord Chancellor to confer on him a knighthood. Two years later the Duke of York, later King James VII, stayed at Bell's Saltmarket house when he visited Glasgow.

There was a flesh market in the area 10 years before the street opened, which was the main place to buy butcher meat in the city. *The Herald,* or, as it was then, *The Herald & Advertiser,* was printed for 22 years at 6d a copy in Bell Street, (Glasgow Herald Close) which was also the home of the second Glasgow Police Office, one stair up.

Bell Street 1876, drawn by David Small.

Nothing exists of the original street and nearly all the late Victorian warehouses have been converted into flats.

Bell o' the Brae (T/head)

In Scottish language the Bell o' the Brae is a term applied to the highest part of the slope of a hill, 'bel' signifying a prominence.

The name is rarely used in Glasgow today, but in the 13th and 14th centuries it was the most important spot in Glasgow — at the intersection of High Street with the Drygate and Rottenrow where the Market Cross stood. Dangerously steep in early times,

Bell o' the Brae.

the ascent was lowered in 1783 to make the Cathedral more accessible to churchgoers. Over the years more was sliced off the top causing the removal of many picturesque wooden houses that fronted the street.

Glasgow's first battle took place at the Bell o' the Brae. Around 1300 there was an English garrison in the Bishop's Castle at the top of High Street. Sir William Wallace attacked the Castle and the English chased him down High Street, but just there, as planned, the Scots turned to fight. Another Scottish force, led by Wallace's uncle, Auchinleck, came up the Drygate and attacked from the rear. The English, hemmed in back and front were defeated. Some cast doubt on the authenticity of this tale, but all histories of Glasgow include it.

Burnet & Boston's 1901 competition winning, red sandstone, crow-stepped tenements that sweep majestically round into Duke/George Streets replaced the old thatched, wooden houses.

Blackader Aisle (C/dral)

Named after Glasgow's first Archbishop, Robert Blackader, who in 1488 obtained a Bull from Pope Alexander VI raising the See of Glasgow into an Archbishopric settling the vexatious question

Seal of Robert Blackader AD 1500 — Blackader's Crypt, Cathedral.

of English domination by the Archbishop of York. A favourite of King James IV, he helped negotiate a marriage between the King and Margaret Tudor, daughter of England's Henry VII. On 8 August 1503, he performed the wedding ceremony at Holyrood Abbey — the union of 'The Thistle and the Rose'.

Matters of state successfully concluded, Blackader turned his energies towards the Cathedral. He created the exquisitely vaulted great aisle to the south, first known as Fergus Aisle, then Blackader's, also the beautiful rood-screen (arch between nave and choir) with its richly moulded door and sculptured figures depicting the seven ages of man. Old age occupies the centre; infancy, youth and manhood are on the north, with the schoolboy, the lover and the sage on the south. Carvings on the bosses in the crypt's interior show the arms of Blackader and King James and a royal crown with the initial M for Queen Margaret. Archbishop Blackader died on 28 July 1508, *en route* to Jerusalem on a pilgrimage to the Holy Grave.

Blackfriars Street (m/c)

Takes its name from the Dominicans, or Black Friars, who around 1240 founded a monastery on the east side of High Street. They

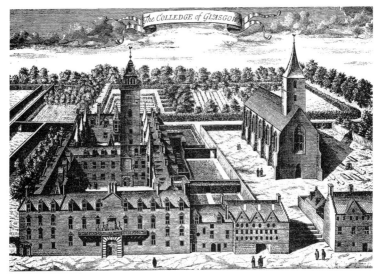

Old College and Blackfriars Church.

built a handsome church with a steeple, fitted up in 1603 as a prison for ecclesiastical offenders who were 'steepled' and fed on bread and water. The church, which survived the Reformation, was gifted to the adjoining University but got into disrepair and was handed back to the City. Badly damaged by lightning on 29 October 1670, it was taken down and replaced twenty years later by the 'College Church' which was demolished when the University moved to Gilmorehill.

Blackfriars Street, or Wynd, has existed since 1400, but not always in the same location. It was originally on the east side of High Street alongside Blackfriars Church, but railway development swallowed it up. Happily only the street vanished, not the name. It moved directly across the road to what had been Stirling Street, planned by John Stirling in 1797 on the large plot of land behind his family's High Street tenement. He commissioned architect James Adam to design houses, shops and warehouses within palace frontages. Stirling also planned a square, unsuccessfully, as he failed to acquire some essential property. Destroyed by the City Improvement Trust, all that survives of Stirling Street is the building renovated in 1986 that houses 'Babbity Bowster's' bistro, said to have been the Kings Head Inn patronised by nobility and gentry in the L8th century.

Blythswood Square (comm/c)

Blythswood must be the wood of Blyth — who or what Blyth was I am unable to discover, but the area at one time was part of the Bishop's Forest. Forest does not always denote a wood; it can signify land set apart for game, like a deer forest. Blythswood Square (1823) on the crown of Blythswood Hill, was originally Garden Square, after developer Hamilton William Garden. It was said he cut off at least thirty feet from the top of the hill to form the square. When he went bankrupt and fled to the USA, others finished the project. Architect John Brash's square consisted of four identical late classical terraces of white dressed ashlar stone (squared stones in regular rows) facing a central garden.

In 1908 the Lady Artists' Club embellished No. 5 with a Charles Rennie Macintosh door inset. No. 7 was the home of the notorious, Madeleine Smith, accused in 1857 of poisoning her lover Pierre Emile L'Angelier. To the charge of murder the jury returned a 'Not Proven' verdict.

Bridge of Sighs (N/lis)

In 1831 it was decided to build a bridge over the Molendinar Burn at the foot of Kirk Street to

> afford a proper entrance to the new cemetery, combining convenient access to the grounds with suitable decoration to the venerable Cathedral and surrounding scenery, to unite the tombs of many generations who have gone before with the resting places destined for generations yet unborn, where the ashes of all shall repose until the resurrection of the just.

For the laying of the foundation stone on 18 October 1833, a platform was erected on the Molendinar's east bank to accommodate Provost Ewing, clergymen, members of the Merchant House (who built the Necropolis), assorted dignitaries and Mr Orme's Cathedral Band. Spectators occupied the west side. After all and sundry had sung part of the 90th psalm and an impressive prayer had been offered, James Hutcheson, Dean of Guild laid the stone.

West side of Blythswood Square.

Bridge of Sighs, when built.

Designed by James and David Hamilton, the bridge, a Roman arch with a 60-feet span, built chiefly of stone from Milton Quarry, cost £1,240. It was called the Bridge of Sighs. No, not after the famous bridge in Venice, but appropriately because of all the funeral parties that crossed over it — how many were in tears? Under the bridge was another small and ancient arch, believed to be one of the oldest pieces of masonry in the city, going back possibly to the time when the earliest parts of the Cathedral were built.

The bridge's construction improved the church road through the valley, an iron railing erected on the cemetery side providing an excellent fence without obstructing the view of the Necropolis.

Bridgegate (S/mkt)

In 1100 it was a track leading to a bridge over the River Clyde. When Bishop Rae around 1350 erected the first stone bridge at the foot of Stockwell which replaced the old 'Brig of Tree' referred to in Wallace's time, the track became known as Bridgegate, or 'Briggait' as it was popularly called — the road to the bridge. Bridgegate was the connection with Glasgow Bridge from Saltmarket, and was once the city's most fashionable thoroughfare. There, rich 17th-century merchants built their houses, including Campbell of Blythswood whose property looked very similar to a neighbouring building where all the great assemblies and balls were held. It was the Merchants Hall (1651) whose steeple was topped with a weathervane of a merchant ship which symbolically sailed to 'a' the airts the wind can blaw'.

For over 100 years Bridgegate remained a desirable neighbourhood. However, the erection in 1744 of the first public slaughterhouses (where the High Court now stands) and later an old clothes' market in Scanlon's Close on the street's south side did not exactly enhance the area. After the Merchants' House was demolished in 1818, except the steeple, which later adorned the fishmarket, it went rapidly downhill. By the 1840s it had become one of the city's most congested and unattractive spots. Some merchant's old mansion houses were still standing, but empty. Squatters, Irish immigrants, moved in, and before long the once fashionable

Engraving by Joseph Swan of Bridgegate, showing old Merchants House steeple.

thoroughfare had become an Irish quarter. There was the O'Doughterty lodging house, the Kelly spirit cellar, Finnigan's second-hand jewellery shop and James Lynch's undertaking establishment. The Londonderry Hotel catered for orangemen and the Emerald Isle Tavern for Catholics. At times the district was extremely volatile, especially on Saturday nights, when the sight of an orange flower or ribbon was all that was needed to start a battle.

The arrival of the Union Railway in 1864 produced a radical change. The slaughterhouses and old clothes' market were among the first removals, and open spaces began to replace crowded buildings. Subsequent railway building (a bridge over the area) combined with the Corporation's project to rid the city of insanitary buildings and to widen streets, reduced Bridgegate to a shadow of its former self.

Bridgeton

In 1705 John Walkinshaw laid off for feuing part of the Barrowfield lands called Goosefaulds. However, only 19 lots were taken up in 19 years, and the whole was sold in 1731 to John Orr, after whom Orr Street was named. The place was of no account until the bridge over the Clyde uniting it with Rutherglen was built in 1775 along with a new road (Main Street). Within a couple of years the village of Barrowfield had adopted a new name, Bridgetown (later Bridgeton).

After David Dale and George Mackintosh set up the Barrowfield Dyeworks in 1785, the open green spaces vanished as Bridgeton developed rapidly into an industrial village, with particular emphasis on the cotton trade. Street names reminiscent of Bridgeton's past glory still exist — Muslin, Poplin, Mill and Landressy, which should be 'Landres' after a small French village that had been the hometown of a Turkey Red Dye operative who built the first house in the street. Housing for working people appeared, mainly tenements built on a grid plan the first of which was on the site of today's Bridgeton Cross Mansions. The present 'Bridgeton Cross' is not the original. That was exactly where Dale and Reid Streets crossed and was for years marked by a sunken cross in the road surface.

During the first half of the L9th century Bridgeton was famed for its tea gardens landscaped with promenades and leafy bowers where visitors could enjoy tea, coffee, strawberries and cream, or, for those who preferred stronger fare, the best spirits and liqueurs. In 1830, the Swan Tavern and Tea Garden at 182 Main Street, had the first zoo in Glasgow, and people flocked to view the animals.

Bridgeton has the largest Burns Club in the world, founded in 1870. In 1874 it held a competition among the local schools for

Corner of Main Street Bridgeton/Dalmarnock Road. The house stood at the junction of the two roads which led respectively to the Rutherglen Bridge and the Dalmarnock Bridge and was the first tenement built in Bridgeton. Bridgeton Cross Mansions took its place.

the best rendering of Burns's works in the form of solo and choir singing and recitations.

In 1900 Alexander Govan produced the first Argyle cars in Hozier Street (a couple of which are on show in the Transport Museum) and in 1906 Singer manufactured sewing machines in James Street. When production moved to Clydebank, the Bridgeton workers were transported there on a train known as 'The Singer Special'.

Celtic Football Club was founded in 1888 in St Mary's Halls, Orr Street, by Marist brother, Walfrid. Initially, the main function of forming the club was to raise funds to provide meals for needy children in the city's east end.

A well-known landmark at Bridgeton Cross is 'The Umbrella', a gift in 1874 from George Smith & Co of the Sun Foundry. A cast iron shelter, it has a red slated roof, a square clock tower and a whimsical weathervane.

Broomielaw (River)

A bush conferred its name on Glasgow's first harbour.

BROOMIELAW — a grassy slope or meadow with broom growing on it. The Campus de Bromilaw was first mentioned about 1325. About 1556 the removal of a ford and sandbanks enabled small craft to reach the Broomielaw. There was no harbour; vessels simply moored in mid-stream. In 1663 'ane litle Key was builded with oak taken from the Cathedral with weigh-hous, fountain and cran'. It is often taken for granted that the site of the quay was settled by its being below the Jamaica Bridge. However, there was no bridge until 1772. The 'wee key' changed the rustic appearance of the Broomielaw Croft where the golden blossoms of the broom waved luxuriantly. A new harbour was built in 1688 at a cost of £1,666.13.4d, which was said to be 'so large that a regiment of horses may be exercised thereon'. At first it extended only to Robertson Street, then to York Street and eventually to its present extent. (The Kingston Bridge).

At the top of the harbour was a series of broad steps. There, the herring boats arrived and when they did 'Bell Geordie' paraded the streets loudly proclaiming 'fresh herrings, Lochfyne herrings, just arrived at the Broomielaw'. On this announcement crowds of people flocked to the steps to hand over sixpence for a dozen. Crowds also flocked to the harbour in 1806 to witness the arrival of a schooner direct from Lisbon, laden with oranges, almonds, figs etc, the first vessel to cross the Atlantic to the Broomielaw. 1812, and the first steamboat left the harbour — Henry Bell's *Comet*.

The Broomielaw developed into a thriving, bustling waterfront lined with tall shipping orientated buildings — Clyde Navigation Trust and the Sailor's Home with its square tower at one end and circular campanile at the other. Often, two of three tiers of shipping lay alongside each other all jostling for a berth. Ships increased in size and business moved down river, but paddle steamers still crowded the Broomielaw 'trips down the water' being one of Glaswegians' favourite recreations. At the height of summer 40/50 steamers a day left the Broomielaw. Sailings stopped from there

Busy bustling Broomielaw in 1870, showing first stage in the construction of Central Station railway bridge, sailing ships, paddle steamers, loading sheds, horses and carts, carriages, and teeming with people — a far cry from today's empty riverside!

when Bridge Wharf opened in 1927. Today the occasional visit of PS Waverley is the last reminder of yesteryear.

Brown Street (B/law)

Brown Street, built on the Broomielaw Croft, was named after the village of Brownfield, which in turn was named after its founder, John Brown, senior partner of Brown Carrick & Co, muslin and lawn manufacturers, who used the ground as his bleaching field.

Along the banks of the river were elegant villas whose owners sent their horses to the fields for exercising. In 1775 locals were forced to ask them not to allow their servants to ride through the villages in such crowds or at such great speed, as the bleaching fields were being ruined from the dust sent up by flying hooves. They also feared for their lives through number and fury of the riders.

Brown's mansion on the south side of Anderston Walk (Argyle Street) was tenanted at the beginning of the L9th century by the artist, John Knox, famous for his panoramic paintings of battles and foreign cities exhibited (1825–26) in a large round wooden pavilion on the west side of Buchanan Street. His painting of the Trongate (1826) has hung in the People's Palace almost without a break since 1898.

Buccleuch Street (G/hill)

There is nothing special about the street named after the Duke of Buccleuch, but there is about No. 145, now a museum — The National Trust for Scotland's Tenement House. In 1911, twenty-five-year-old Agnes Toward and her mother moved in, and there spinster Agnes spent the rest of her life. When she died and the flat was sold it was discovered that over the years Agnes had changed nothing in her home. As well as her special treasures, she had kept old letters, postcards and all sorts of trivia which, with the furniture and fittings, give a wonderfully intimate insight into life at the time.

Buchanan Street (c/c)

The locality that became Buchanan Street was entirely rural and considered 'too far west' for development. However, the man after whom it was named was a man of vision who believed the city would spread in that direction.

In 1766 Tobacco Merchant Andrew Buchanan bought four acres of land reaching from Argyle Street up to the Meadowflat Lands (Gordon Street) and built a mansion house at what is now the south-west corner of Buchanan Street. He decided to feu a street and advertised land for sale. A tenement was erected opposite his house in 1778, the space between eventually forming the street. Unfortunately Andrew got no further with his plan as the revolt of the American colonies bankrupted him. However, his trustees carried out the scheme, and in 1780 opened Buchanan Street.

Early in the L9th century it was a thoroughfare mainly of villas and farms and did not become commercial until 1828 when the

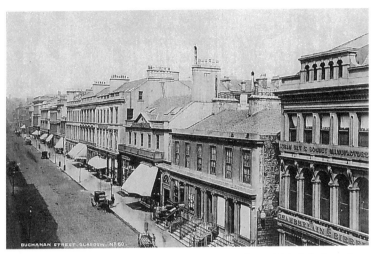

Buchanan Street in 1868. At first it was purely residential then shops appeared. A carriage stands outside the Arcade, the low building, being the original one that fronted it. To its left is Prince of Wales Building, now Princes Square and to its right a building just about to be demolished. Wylie Hill's store occupied the new building that burned down in 1888. However, when rebuilt the firm remained in situ until the 1970s when high rating forced it out of business.

Argyll Arcade was built. The first house (1778) was on the east side of the street, a handsome pedimented villa, whose garden, in 1837, was the venue for the famous Peel Banquet. For the occasion an enormous wooden pavilion was temporarily erected, said to be without parallel in Great Britain. Sadly, the house was demolished in 1842 to make room for the Prince of Wales Building and Square, a courtyard of business chambers. In 1987 the court was roofed, and Princes Square, an upmarket shopping centre, was created.

Buchanan Street's first great building was St. George's Church (1807) designed by Wm. Stark. It had a steeple 162½ feet high and a bell bearing the inscription 'I to the Church the people call, and to the grave I summon all'. The street has its share of architectural gems: Royal Bank of Scotland (1850), Stock Exchange (1875), old Glasgow Herald Office (1879), Athenaeum Theatre (1891); but its real claim to fame was as Glasgow's élitist shopping area. The

North Buchanan Street before it was developed.

city's best known stores — Fraser's, Wylie & Lochhead, Macdonalds, Wylie Hills (all gone bar Frasers) were there.

When Chemists, Frazer & Green, opened their shop in 1830 at No. 105 (facing what's now Exchange Place) grass was still growing luxuriantly in the upper part of the street and business was anything but brisk. In fact sales for the whole of July were under £17. Then, the Buchanan Street Hotel, with a large walled garden filled with apple and pear trees and a conservatory where grapes grew, stood where Fraser's main door now is.

In 1847, at No. 19, Sturrocks celebrated the opening of their hairdressing establishment bizarrely. They put on public view the carcass of a bear and so great were the crowds the police were called in. Bear's grease was the Victorian 'Brylcreem'. At No. 49 in the 1880s, furrier George Sieber offered to remodel sealskin jackets to current styles, and at No. 152 Paterson Sons & Co, published *The Vocal Melodies of Scotland, the Best and Most Complete Edition of Scotch Songs*. Opticians and photographers, Lizars, settled into their present premises in 1892.

No history of Buchanan Street would be complete without mention of tearooms — Stuart Cranston, the pioneer of the tearoom, had his above the Arcade entrance, and his sister, Kate, had hers at No. 91, a delightful, decorative piece of architecture by George Washington Browne.

Buck's Head Buildings (Argyle Street c/c)

From the Buck's Head Hotel that originally occupied the site at the corner of Argyle/Dunlop Streets. Built in 1750 of fine light sandstone with a double sided stairway, it was the first mansion in Argyle Street and the home of Provost John Murdoch. Converted into an inn in 1790 its sign was a gilt stag's head, complete with horns. Many distinguished guests stayed there, including Thomas Telford and Sir Walter Scott, who was not over impressed with his accommodation. On leaving he commented to friends that he was on his way to visit Colonel Campbell's Blythswood House, both grand and comfortable where the sleep at night will make amends for the Buck's Head.

Alexander 'Greek' Thomson's Buck's Head Building, an iron framed warehouse with windows fitted directly into the pilasters replaced the inn in 1862. At the apex, a sculpture of a buck sits on

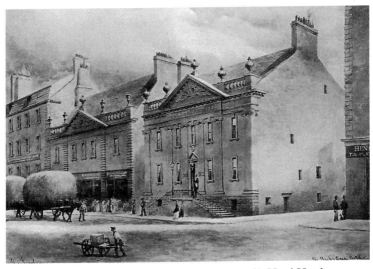

Thomas Fairbairn's picture of the old Buck's Head Hotel.

a plinth inscribed 'BUCK'S HEAD BUILDINGS'. In the 1980s the building was narrowly saved from the same fate as Provost Murdoch's mansion — demolition.

Cadogan Street (B/law)

After Henry Cadogan, commander of the 71st Light Infantry, commonly known as 'The Glasgow Regiment', stationed at Gallowgate Barracks. On its way to fight in the Peninsular Campaigns, the regiment, clad in tartan trews and highland bonnets, marched out of the barracks under the command of Lieut-Col Cadogan. Cheering enthusiastically, crowds of people accompanied them for miles.

At the bloody Battle of Vittoria (1813) against the French in Northern Spain, the regiment was hard pressed, but brave Cadogan spurred them on with the rallying cry 'Seventy First, down the Gallowgate with them'. It worked. To the skirl of the pipes the men advanced and played a full part in a great military victory. The enemy lost all their artillery, field equipment and treasure chest and King Joseph (Napoleon's brother) narrowly escaped capture. The French were broken and driven out of the country.

Many brave Gallowgate lads fell with their gallant Colonel, and in the Nave of Glasgow Cathedral there is a monumental tablet to Cadogan recording his valour:

> Sacred to the memory of the Honourable Henry Cadogan, Lieut-Colonel of the 71st, or Glasgow Regiment, who gloriously fell at the head of his battalion in the ever-memorable Battle of Vittoria June 21st 1813, aged 33. This monument is erected by a few of his friends in this city and neighbourhood to perpetuate the remembrance of his worth as a man and his gallantry as a soldier.

Ca'd'Oro (c/c)

Some say the name derives from Venice's celebrated Golden House, *Casa d'Oro,* others that it came from the restaurant inserted in the 1920s. Regardless of how it came by its name, John Honeyman's building of 1872, designed as a furniture warehouse,

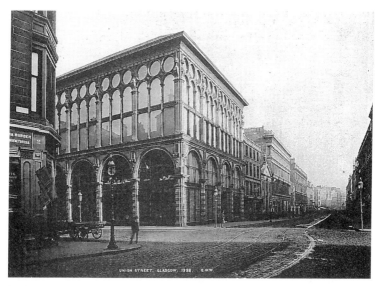

This early view of Union Street, taken looking south, shows the Ca'd'Oro not long after its completion in 1872. It must have been taken early in the morning, as apart from one horse and cart, a boy and a man, the place is devoid of people or traffic. Note the tram lines which were laid in the same year as the Ca'd'Oro was built.

was a magnificent cast iron palazzo. Above the giant stone-arched shopfronts were triple arched cast-iron bays embellished with decorative mouldings. Circular attic windows were crowned by a concave cornice.

In 1921 the City Bakeries opened its magnificent restaurant complex in a Ca'd'Oro sumptuously refurbished by J Gaff Gillespie, one of Glasgow's most *avant garde* architects. A marble faced hall housing artistic confectionery and tobacco kiosks gave separate access to the restaurant floors. Downstairs was the smoke room and something new — a 'quick service' lunch counter decorated with a view of Venice, a theme continued in the first floor 'Venetian Tea Room'. The banqueting hall, later designated a Ballroom, was on the newly-added 5th floor. In its heyday the Ca'd'Oro was Glasgow's 'in' place and a popular wedding venue until superseded in 1950s by the Grosvenor in Gordon Street.

Stakis took over parts of the Ca'd'Oro in the 1960s as restaurants — The Brasserie, El Guero, and The Tropicana.

A great fire in 1987 reduced the building to a shell, which, in a roundabout way, was a blessing, as the ugly mansard roof added in 1922 was destroyed. When the building was reconstructed it was to its former glory, even better, with the addition of two replica end-bays to Union Street replacing the 1920s Art Deco extension by Jack Coia.

Calton

A 'hazel grove', or from the Gaelic word *Coillduin* meaning 'wood on the hill'.

John Walkinshaw purchased the lands of Barrowfield from the Council in 1705. He feud part of the ground (East Blackfaulds) into a small weavers' village just outside Glasgow's east boundary and outside the jurisdiction of its guilds. The Council bought Barrowfield back in 1723 and Blackfaulds became Calton. The village, situated between Gallowgate and Barrowfield Road (London Road), had three streets intersected by a Cross. Main Street ran north and south, High Street east and New Street west to Glasgow's boundary. Calton Entry (near Barrowland Ballroom) connected Calton to Gallowgate.

Calton's Coat of Arms shows its weaving connections, three cats with shuttles in their mouths, a shuttle being a weaver's tool.

King Street, Calton, drawn by David Small in the 1880s. With its white-washed walls, red pantiled roofs and red chimneys, Calton was unique among Glasgow's villages.

Merchant John Orr bought the estate in 1730. Five years later King George II made it a Barony, giving Orr the right to make laws and punish those who broke them. Calton had a Baron's jail with iron-stanchioned windows.

As Gallowgate spread east, so did Calton. A new village was added to the old and another entry made from Gallowgate (Calton Mouth) into what is now Bain Square. By 1788 both villages reached Barrowfield Road and the hamlet of Mile-end (north of Bridgeton Cross).

Calton became a burgh in 1815 with a provost, three bailies, a treasurer and eleven councillors. Two years later it had its own police force and had annexed the village of Mile-end. Independence ended in 1846 when it became part of Glasgow.

Tureen Street in Calton, (from the French *terrine,* an earthen vessel) had several potteries, one belonging to Catholic Robert Bagnall. In 1779, at the time of the anti-popery demonstrations orchestrated from London by Lord George Gordon, a mob destroyed his home and factory for no lesser a crime than allowing his employees to work on a Kirk fast day. Later the Council compensated him.

Calton is ever identified with weaving, and the history of its weavers is turbulent, the strike of 1787 being the most notable event. Manufacturers cut weavers' wages and threatened that more cuts would follow. On 30 June 1787, thousands of weavers from the West of Scotland met on Glasgow Green and agreed not to accept starvation wages. Employers retaliated by locking them out. The strike dragged on for two months, by which time some weavers were in such dire straits that they gave in. In an attempt to stop the blacklegs working, strikers cut the webs from their looms and publicly burned them. On 3 September the magistrates and military confronted a mob of weavers burning some webs at the Drygate. The weavers rioted, but despite the reading of the Riot Act they refused to disperse and the soldiers were ordered to fire. Three men were killed on the spot and several others were wounded. Six thousand people attended the shot weavers' funerals in the newly created Calton Burial Ground. Their grave was marked by a large flat stone bearing the inscription:

> This is the property of the weaving body under the charge of the five districts of Calton, erected by them to the memory of John Page, Alexander Miller and James Ainsley, who, at a meeting of that body for resisting the reduction of their wages, were upon the third day of September 1787, martyred by the military under orders of the Civic Authority of Glasgow firing upon the multitude.

Candleriggs (m/c)

As with some other old city streets, there is more than one version of how Candleriggs got its name. However, the one most frequently mentioned is that there were candleworks near Ramshorn Church and the street was laid out over the 'riggs' or ridges of croft lands on which they had been built. Hence Candleriggs. An interesting interpretation turned up in the *Evening Citizen* of 22 June 1936 by courtesy of a reader:

> When the Ramshorn Church stood among fields, the then minister was a good weather prophet and on one occasion he told his people

Old Map.

to gather in the corn, for although there was no sign of approaching bad weather, he predicted a severe storm. The taking in of the corn began, and the people worked into the night by the aid of lanterns lit by candles. From that time the field was known as 'Candleriggs'.

Version one sounds more feasible as there were candle works on the site, but it's nice to have a choice.

After the great fire of 1652 the city fathers prohibited candle making in houses. This paved the way for a new industry and in 1658 the Council granted permission to built candle factories. For safety these were kept well away from the city's buildings and erected on the 'townes rig' six score ells (an ell = 37 inches) to the west of the thorn hedges of the Flesh Market in High Street (north end of Candleriggs). Slowly the street evolved through the area until completed around 1720.

Candleriggs in the 18th century was a very different place from today. The guard house was at the south west corner; then came

Candleriggs

the herb market, weigh house and meal market. At the north east corner was a candle and soap factory that burned down in 1771. The first issue of the *Glasgow Courant,* 11 November 1715, advertised that 'Anyone who wants good black or speckled soap may be served by Robert Luke, Manager of the Soaperie of Glasgow at reasonable rates'. The Western and North Sugar Houses were at the corner of Candleriggs/Bell Street. Between the soap and sugar works was a walled bowling green which stayed verdant until city smoke stopped the grass from growing.

In 1817 a bazaar, designed by James Clelland, with stances for groceries, fruit, cheese, poultry, game, second hand books, toys — in fact practically everything — was built on the bowling green ground. It was remodelled in 1886 and again in the 1840s when the City Hall was added to it. Miscellaneous trading ceased, and by 1914 it had become the main market in the West of Scotland for fruit and vegetables. Merchandise was sold by auction and sales were held daily during the height of the fruit season. The fruit market moved to Blochairn in 1969.

Carrick Street (B/law)

Named after Robin Carrick, junior partner in Brown & Carrick, muslin and lawn manufacturers, who had their business in the Broomielaw. However, his main claim to fame was as the skinflint, miserly chief of The Ship Bank, Glasgow's first indigenous bank.

Carrick, although revered by the financial community for his business acumen, was not liked. One of Glasgow's greatest misers, his frugal and miserable way of living was unworthy of a man of his standing. Although from a comparatively poor background he managed to amass an immense fortune of nearly a million pounds — unimaginable riches then.

A dour joyless bachelor, he lived in a flat above the bank at the south-west corner of Glassford/Argyle Streets along with Miss Paisley, his spinster niece and housekeeper. They were well matched, she being as miserable as he was in fact, more so. She was often seen haggling and bartering with shopkeepers in King Street, then the main provisions quarter, to bring down the price of a piece of beef or mutton.

On the rare occasions when auld Robin entertained, Miss Paisley went to Caldwell's provision shop in Glassford Street to 'borrow' a large Gouda cheese, explaining that although neither she nor the banker ate such a delicacy it had to be available for guests. It was weighed, and on return she paid for as many ounces as had been eaten. The arrangement was similar with the greengrocer. She took back any choice apples or pears not eaten and got her money refunded.

Robin Carrick.

In the disastrous year 1793, three Glasgow banks failed with even the great Royal Bank trembling. One major bank alone, The Ship, ignored the panic and carried on, firm as a rock. Although criticised for being hard, unyielding, and unsympathetic, its boss kept his head, never wavering and his bank survived the crisis.

Castle Street (C/dral)

No prizes for guessing how it got its name (1100) — the way to the Bishop's Castle or Palace, used for either purpose as the exigencies of war or religion demanded. It stood in the region of the Royal Infirmary. When John Baliol was King of Scotland, Edward I of England had a small garrison of soldiers quartered in the castle. It was this garrison that William Wallace tried to dislodge (*circa* 1300) in the first battle fought in Glasgow's streets at the Bell o'the'Brae.

Engraving showing Castle and Cathedral.

Around 1438 Bishop Cameron added a great tower, and about 1510 Archbishop Beaton built a 15-foot-high fortified wall, a bastion, ditch and tower. Archbishop Dunbar built the last addition around 1530, a gatehouse. In 1544, the Earl of Lennox's men garrisoned the castle. The Earl of Arran, who acted as regent during the minority of Queen Mary, besieged it for ten days. The garrison surrendered under promise of mercy which was not honoured. Arran hanged sixteen of the defenders at the Cross (then at the intersection of Rottenrow/Drygate). This treachery led to the Battle of the Butts, which Arran won.

In 1752 a mob of religious zealots, who regarded it as 'the devil's house' destroyed Glasgow's first theatre, a ramshackle booth built against a wall of the castle. The Archbishops fled their palace at the start of the Reformation (1560). Around 1576 the Town Council transferred its meetings from the castle to the old Tolbooth at the foot of High Street. With the departure of the Archbishops and Council, the ancient pile went downhill until it reached the status of a prison, at one time housing three hundred Jacobite prisoners. By the mid 18th century it was almost a quarry, and when Archbishop Dunbar's gateway was demolished in 1755 the Council granted permission to use the masonry for city building projects. In 1784 the castle yard became the place for public executions and on those occasions the ruins thronged with spectators. The final remnants of the castle were cleared in 1792 to make way for Robert Adam's Royal Infirmary.

Cathedral Street

Again no prizes — the way to the Cathedral. Not an ancient thoroughfare as may be expected. Cathedral Street opened in 1840, but prior to then there was a narrow road called Potterow Loan, a short distance south from the present street, which ran in the same direction. Railway development swept it away and altered the locality.

The street may not be ancient but the Cathedral is. In 1124 Glasgow's first Bishop, John Achaius, began to build a Cathedral on the site of St Mungo's wooden church and King David consecrated the partly wooden and stone building on 7 July 1136. Fire destroyed it in 1192, and thanks to the endeavours of Bishop Jocelyn a new Cathedral and tomb to St Mungo were opened on 6 July 1197. Of this church only a single wall-shaft resting upon a fragment of bench-table remains near the south-west entrance to the Lower Church.

The Cathedral building of today was begun by Bishop William de Bondington (1233–1258) who completed the quire and lower church. Bishop Lauder built the steeple up to the battlements in 1425 and laid the foundation of the vestry. His successor, Bishop Cameron, 'The Magnificent', completed the spire, chapterhouse and sacristy as well as building the consistory house and tower. Archbishop Blackader continued to improve the Cathedral by building the great aisle to the south and the rood screen.

Although all the images and altars were destroyed, the fabric of the Cathedral fortunately escaped the excesses of the Reformation. The Trades Guilds deserve special tribute, for to them we owe the existence of our finest medieval monument. They saved it from demolition in 1579 by taking arms and declaring to the workmen about to do the deed that 'he who would cast down the first stone shall be buried under it'. Only when the magistrates

Cathedral minus its consistory house but still with tower.

gave the order to down tools did they move. After the Reformation the building was used as three separate parish churches — The Inner High, the Outer High and the Laigh or Barony. Archbishop Spottiswoode began the leaden roof in 1600 and Archbishop Law completed it around 1630.

In an attempt to improve the Cathedral's appearance, or so it was thought, our Victorian city fathers made an ill-judged decision to remove the 15th-century consistory house and tower adjoining the west gable. Citizens, including architects, appealed to the magistrates to halt the destruction of 'one of the ancient landmarks of Glasgow', but to no avail. The consistory house came down in 1846 and the tower in 1848. Another act of wanton vandalism by the powers that be.

Cathedral Street is now an educational thoroughfare. It is surrounded by seats of learning, the University of Strathclyde campus on the right and other colleges on the left.

Charlotte Street (C/ton)

Named in honour of Queen Charlotte, George III's consort, and once occupied by rented out gardens called 'dails', the rent for each being one merk per day. Consequently, the district became known as Merkdaily.

Archibald Paterson and his partner David Dale, 'father of the Scottish Cotton Industry', laid out Charlotte Street in 1779 on the site of the abandoned St James Square. This once delightful street ran north and south between Glasgow Green and the Gallowgate, intersected by London Road. North Charlotte Street was designed as a tenement development for artisans but South Charlotte Street boasted elegant mansions each with its own coach house and garden. At the Green end elegant railings and a locked gate cut it off from traffic.

Dale's own mansion was at the south-west corner. Said to be designed by Robert Adam, it cost £6,000 to build in 1782. Unfortunately, the setting was not always idyllic, as the Camlachie Burn running nearby often overflowed. Once when Dale had invited a large group of wealthy VIPs to dinner, it rose to an unusual height, burst into his kitchen, put the fires out, and made the servants run for their lives. Not an enviable situation with guests soon to arrive. But all was not lost, help was on hand. Good neighbours, unaffected by the deluge, came to the rescue by lending their kitchens and servants. The dinner party went ahead on schedule and was a great success.

In 1850 the mansion became the city's Eye Infirmary, and the oculist Dr William McKenzie carried out operations in David Dale's delightful octagonal study. The house was demolished in 1954 to make way for an extension to Our Lady and St Francis' school. Again, an example of Glasgow's cavalier attitude to its historic buildings.

St Aloysius College began in Charlotte Street directly across from Dale's house. Later R Paterson & Sons, famous for 'Camp Coffee', Britain's first instant coffee, occupied the site. The company boasted that a single cup or a gallon could be produced at a moment's notice and no matter who made it the quality was always the same.

Charlotte Street, showing the gates that shut it off from Glasgow Green and David Dale's mansion at the southwest corner, which was much more imposing than the others in the street.

All that remains of the original south Charlotte Street is a simple classical villa of two storeys and five bays, unfortunately minus its coach house. North of London Road only one dilapidated artisan's tenement with circular staircase tower remains, No. 24.

Chisholm Street (S/mkt)

This short street leading from Trongate to Parnie Street (which used to be Princes Street and before that Gibson's Wynd) was named after Provost Samuel Chisholm, a native of Dalkeith who came to Glasgow in 1870 and began a wholesale grocery business. A life-long abstainer and well-known as a fervent supporter of the temperance cause, he was instrumental in the Council passing a resolution that no part of its property should be let as public-houses.

Sir Samuel Chisholm's name goes down in municipal history for his tireless work in connection with the City Improvement Trust, formed to clear the city of its slums and provide decent hygienic housing for those of the humbler class at moderate rents.

Sir Samuel Chisholm, Bart.

Being one of the most squalid and insanitary regions in the world, the area around Saltmarket and Trongate was a prime candidate for improvement.

Wide streets, warehouses and comfortable dwelling houses replaced the warren of stinking vennels and wynds with their hovels, shebeens and brothels. One of the new streets was named 'Chisholm' out of respect for the man largely responsible for the neighbourhood's transformation.

The River Clyde

From the Gaelic word *Clith* meaning 'strong'. The noble river, the 'Cluyd' of the ancient Britons, rises from the same range of hills on the borders of Lanarkshire and Dumfriesshire as the Rivers Tweed and Annan. It passes Lanark, Hamilton and Rutherglen before it reaches Glasgow.

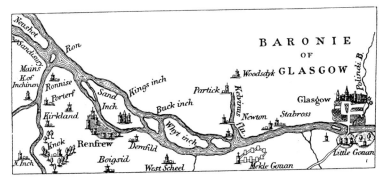

Map of inches.

In early times it was a meandering shallow stream. Glasgow's merchants used Irvine as their shipping port and transported their goods across twenty-five miles of country by pack-horses. As foreign trade escalated the city's distance from the sea was a serious handicap and the Town Council tried to coax the Burgh of Dumbarton into becoming Glasgow's port, which offer they declined 'lest the influx of mariners should raise the price of butter and eggs to the townsmen'. Thus rebuffed, Glasgow purchased a few acres of land eighteen miles down river in 1688 and built a harbour around which a town sprang up — Port Glasgow. While a vast improvement over the previous arrangement, it was still far from perfect. The really desirable thing was to bring the ships to the heart of the city.

Council records mention a proposal for 'taking away the sands stopping the ships and barques from coming to the town', as far back as 1609. The chief obstacle was Dumbuck Ford where the river was only two feet deep at low water. Also in the channel were sandbanks and islands or 'inches' like Kings Inch and Whyt Inch. No real progress was made until 1768 when Chester engineer, John Golborne came up with a plan — throw the current into the centre of the river by means of jetties and help the natural scour of the water further by dredging the channel. It worked. By 1775 the Clyde was navigable and vessels drawing six feet of water were able for the first time at high tide to come up to the Broomielaw. Six years later the depth of water at low tide was fourteen feet and vessels drawing seven feet of water could come up to the Quay.

Over the decades more and more headway was made until the Clyde developed from a mere salmon stream into one of the world's finest waterways and harbours.

Clyde Street

Built on part of Glasgow's Old Green that extended from the Clyde to Argyle Street and from Stockwell Street to Jamaica Street. It was originally known as the Horse Brae from the slope that led to the ford, and because the horse fair was held there every Wednesday. The banqueting room of the City Chambers has a large panel depicting such a fair. The horses were trotted out for inspection in Stockwell, Glassford and Argyle Streets and along the Trongate. Clyde Street (1799) had, and still has, its fair share of impressive buildings.

Before the street was formed the finest Palladian villa in the city was built in 1752, at what is now the corner of Ropework Lane, by Allan Dreghorn, the designer of St Andrew's Church. His nephew, Glasgow's ugliest man, Robert Dreghorn (nicknamed Bob Dragon) inherited the house. So ugly was Bob that mothers used him as a bogeyman to frighten their children into behaving. Nevertheless, his hideous appearance did not stop Bob admiring the fair sex, and he never lost an opportunity to pursue the beauties who caught his fancy. Quite understandably they all rebuffed his advances. One day in 1806 Bob could take no more. He committed suicide, and henceforth his mansion was said to be haunted. Carrick Quay occupies the site.

To the mansion's left was the Town's Hospital or poorhouse, built by the Town Council, General Session, Trades' House and Merchants' House in 1773, to provide the poor with wholesome food, good clothes and clean lodgings at low cost. The poorhouse was in front and the infirmary behind, and below that was the Lunatic Asylum.

St Andrew's Roman Catholic Cathedral in Clyde Street is one of the city's much admired architectural treasures. Erected in 1816 at a cost of £16,000 and designed by James Gillespie Graham, it

Engraving by Joseph Swan showing Clyde Street around 1820 with St Andrew's Roman Catholic Cathedral in the centre and the Town Poorhouse and Hospital to its right. The horses and carts show how shallow the river was at that point.

was the first serious piece of Gothic Revivalism in the city. The gable to the street had traceried octagonal buttresses and a niche at the apex containing a statue of St. Andrew.

At 298 Clyde Street can be found the unassuming Greek Doric Customs House built in 1840 by John Taylor, the Irish-born customs official also responsible for Dundee Customs House. Its set back Venetian windowed bays were 20th-century additions, the eastern one linking to a handsomely proportioned five-bay neo-classical block of similar date.

Cochrane Street (m/c)

Opened in 1787 and previously called Cotton Street because it was almost entirely taken up with the offices of cotton workers, spinners and yarn agents. Today, council buildings occupy it. It was named Cochrane Street after Andrew Cochrane, a man of great ability and excellent judgement who thoroughly understood commerce and finance.

Andrew Cochrane.

He was Provost when Prince Charles Edward Stuart and his ragged Highlanders came to the city on Christmas Day 1745. The visit was dreaded with good reason. As Glasgow had prospered under Hanovarian rule its allegiance was not to the Pretender. In fact it had demonstrated its loyalty to the Crown by raising two battalions of volunteers (twelve hundred men) to fight against him. Also, it had only paid part of the £15,000 extortion money demanded by the Jacobites. Glasgow had managed to raise £5,000 by collecting what they could and borrowing the rest. Provost Cochrane summed up public feeling perfectly when he said 'our case is deplorable that we must truckle to a pretender prince and rebel and at an expense we are not able to bear to purchase protection from plunder and rapine'.

Fortunately, thanks to Andrew Cochrane's commendable courage and diplomacy there was no trouble, although as a Whiggish

The quaint house with the gable to the pavement was a 'herb ale house' and in 1885 was the only building remaining of the original Cochrane Street.

bastion (those who were for the Hanoverians) Glasgow could have been sacked and burned. However, it was compelled to accommodate, clothe and feed the six-thousand-strong army. Provost Cochrane was fined £500 for refusing to divulge who had subscribed to the Glasgow Regiment. When the Prince left ten days later he bitterly remarked that nowhere had he found so few friends. According to Cochrane the only recruit found in Glasgow was 'ane Drunken Shoemaker'. A fortnight later Glasgow's volunteers took part in the Battle of Falkirk. Twenty-two were killed, eleven wounded and fourteen taken prisoner.

All told, Glasgow's enforced contribution to the Jacobite cause amounted to over £14,000 which Provost Cochrane tried to retrieve. In 1749 Parliament granted the city £10,000, leaving it £4,000 out of pocket, and the Provost £472.11.8½, as compensation for their losses.

Cochrane, on being asked to what he attributed the sudden rise of Glasgow in his time, said it was 'all owing to four young men of talent and spirit, whose success set an example to others'. The four were: William Cunninghame, Alexander Speirs, John Glassford and James Ritchie, the chiefs of the famous Tobacco Lords.

Andrew's views and commercial experiences were of invaluable help to his great friend Adam Smith while writing *The Wealth of Nations*, probably the most important book on political economy published.

There's a monument to Andrew Cochrane, described as Glasgow's greatest Lord Provost, in the Cathedral.

Collins Street (T/head)

After another Glasgow worthy, William Collins, head of the outstandingly successful publishing business founded by his father in 1819. The Collins family were founder members of Britain's first temperance society, and William's devotion to the campaign for total abstinence earned him the nickname 'Water Willie'.

A typical Victorian Scottish businessman, William devoted time and energy to civic and philanthropic work as well as to making his fortune. Sadly, as a public figure people saw him as a gaunt, stern old Puritan. On becoming Lord Provost in 1877 he came up with a revolutionary, if not exactly popular, way of saving public funds conveniently fitting in with his principles — he only had iced water served for refreshments at civic functions!

During Collins's Provostship two catastrophic events happened. In 1878 The City of Glasgow Bank collapsed, ruining investors and shareholders. William immediately set up a relief fund and from his own pocket made the first substantial contribution. A year later the Tay Rail Bridge fell, plunging the Edinburgh to Dundee express and all its passengers into the water. None escaped to tell the tale.

Collins was a member of the city's College Free Church and a driving force in the Working Men's Evangelistic Association formed in 1869 to bring about 'the religious and moral improvement of the working classes'. In summer, meetings were held in a marquee on Glasgow Green (hence the origin of Tent Hall). He took an active interest in young people's organisations and financially helped a member of his church, William Smith,

Provost William Collins.

become full-time leader of the world's first uniformed youth movement, the Boys Brigade.

William Collins is buried in the Necropolis. Even in death he was not far from his great printing empire in Cathedral Street. In Glasgow Green opposite the High Court, a drinking fountain (a girl with a pitcher) commemorates his work for the temperance cause.

Cowcaddens

A tricky one this. The origin of the name is lost in the mists of time, but most people believe it derived from being the place where the cows were milked. However, on investigation it appears to be a popular misconception. The word Cowcaddens has been spelt in many ways — 1509 Kowcaldens, 1521 Kowkaldens, 1543 Cowkalldens and so on until the present form was reached. Two Scottish dialect dictionaries mention that the first syllable cow

Engraving by Joseph Swan of Glasgow Lunatic Asylum. Built 1814, demolished 1908. (Parliamentary Road)

means goblin, the second KALD means unkind, and DEN or its plural DENNES means the home of or homes of. Therefore, the word Cowcaddens means, in early Scots, the home of the unkind or repellent goblins. Town Council records of 1655 state 'the land to lye for the use of the Towne Kye'. As cows were then known as 'kyne' or 'kye' it seems feasible to assume the name Cowcaddens had nothing to do with our four legged friends, as it was in existence long before the town's herd grazed on the land.

In bygone times the district was agricultural land belonging to the church and formed part of the Bishop's Forest. Cromwell entered Glasgow in 1650 via Cowcaddens and the Cow Loan (Queen street) instead of by the Stablegreen Port, as he had been warned that the vaults of the Bishops' Castle by the roadside there had been filled with gunpowder.

There were two farms called Cowcaddens: The Meikle and The Lytle. In 1793 there was a slaughterhouse and a cattle market. The village stood on the south side of the present Cowcaddens Street and later, because of several silk and cotton mills in the neighbourhood, the north side became known as Mylton. The Forth and Clyde Canal (1790) brought prosperity.

With foundries, cotton, silk and flour mills, engineers' shops, sawmills and timber yards, Cowcaddens was a bee-hive of industry. Feuing began in the early L800s.

William Stark's Lunatic Asylum was built in 1810 on what became Parliamentary Road. It embodied ideas very advanced for their day. A central administration block with four wings in the form of a Greek Cross was most original. However, within a generation the asylum was outmoded and it survived as a poorhouse until its demolition in 1908.

Cowcaddens was annexed to the city in 1846. While the City Improvement Trust did good work by clearing the city centre of its disease-ridden slums, it created others. Homes were demolished without making adequate provision for the occupants, mostly of the poorest class, and Cowcaddens, with its influx of outsiders, became a squalid, overcrowded, unhygienic den of iniquity with one of the worst infant mortality rates in the city.

Nineteenth-century Cowcaddens is no more. Comprehensive redevelopment in the 1960s swept away the tenements and factories, and today the roadway dominates the neighbourhood. Sixteen McPhater Street remains as a landmark for travellers from the city centre — a battlemented warehouse built in 1892, later converted into the Orient model lodging house.

Crimea Street (B/law)

No, not to commemorate the Crimean War, but in honour of William Simpson, the famous Crimean War correspondent and painter who was born there.

Lying between McAlpine and Brown Streets it used to be West College Street, formed on the site of a monastic establishment given by the Crown to the College at the Reformation.

Simpson had little formal education and trained as an illustrator with Glasgow lithographers, Allan and Ferguson. Later in London he created scenic impressions of the 1851 Great Exhibition.

When the Crimean War broke out in 1853, Simpson was commissioned to make on-the-spot illustrated reports on the war earning him the nickname 'Crimean Simpson'. His reports and drawings were brutally realistic, not romanticised. They showed

Tenement at corner of Carrick/West College Streets, birthplace of 'Crimea Simpson'; demolished around 1970.

human suffering and mindless destruction of land and buildings. Much of his later life was spent as a roving reporter for the *Illustrated London News*.

Crimea Simpson's birthplace no longer remains, but thankfully many of his original paintings and drawings do. To Glasgow the most important reminders of his artistic skill are his series of drawings 'Glasgow in the Forties', providing a valuable pictorial record of the city at the time. About these drawings he wrote: 'What spot could compare to the place in which one has been born and grown up...to that dear friend I now dedicate these drawings with the well known words — "Let Glasgow Flourish".'

Dalhousie Street (G/hill)

James Andrew Brown-Ramsay, 10th Earl and 1st Marquis of Dalhousie is responsible for this one. British Governor-General of India from 1847 to 1856 he is credited with being the creator of the modern map of India through his annexations of independent

Steep Dalhousie Street in the 1930s. The pretty gabled building at the west corner has gone, as has Karter's Fur shop and their old-fashioned hanging sign in Douglas Street.

provinces, the first being the Punjab in 1849. A firm believer in the moral and material benefits of British rule he took every opportunity to acquire territory and power. It was customary for a ruler without an heir to ask the British Government if they could adopt one. Dalhousie concluded that if permission was refused the State would lapse and become a British possession. By these means he collected Satara, Jhansi and Nagpur. However, his annexation of Oudh entailed grave political danger. As there was an heir, Dalhousie simply accused the ruler of misgovernment and appropriated the State.

Politically his dealings may have been devious but no-one could fault his energetic work on expanding Indian resources and improving social conditions. He constructed roads, put up telegraph wires, opened the Ganges canal, planned railways, developed trade and agriculture, introduced cheap postage, opened the civil service to all natural British subjects, black or white, and opposed female infanticide, suttee and thuggee.

Regrettably, the widespread controversies aroused by his annexation policy, criticised as largely responsible for the Mutiny in 1857, the year after he left India, overshadowed these achievements. Exhausted by years of overwork, he died in 1860 at the age of forty-eight.

Glasgow's first powder magazine, with living quarters for officers and guards who did a week's duty, was built in the area of Dalhousie Street in 1782 and removed in the mid-nineteenth century.

Dixon Street (St/E)

Named after William Dixon, who created at the head of Crown Street in the 1830s the famous Govan Ironworks (better known as 'Dixon's Blazes' because of the flames shooting out from the chimneystacks). He began with five blast furnaces and much of the ironstone used was mined at Polmadie. It was at his works that Bessemer carried out some of his experiments in steel manufacturing and where Siemens's first regenerating furnace was tried out. Among others, Dixon's head cast in stone adorns the Connal building at the corner of West George/Dundas Streets. Colvilles Steel Works took over Dixon's Blazes in 1958 and demolished it in 1960.

This short, unprepossessing thoroughfare connects Howard Street to Clyde Street and has a few yellow stone classical tenements circa 1850s.

Dobbie's Loan (C/caddens)

Originally known as the Common Vennel (public lane) it was in the 16th/17th century a straggling path giving access to the crofts and common pasture (Kowcaldens) on the north-west of the city. It was never an important thoroughfare. On the west side of the common was a highway leading to the town's quarries and another leading to Garscube Ford connecting with the path. Dobbie's Loan got its name from John Dobbie, a carter and burgess who owned land in the 17th century outside the Stable Green Port (from its proximity to the Castle's stables). In 1747 it was decided to widen and improve the path and Dobbie's Loan became a through road from Castle Street to Garscube Road. A map of 1775 shows Dobbie's Loan stopping short of Garscube Road.

Douglas Street (comm/c)

After James Douglas. James Campbell, younger brother of Colin Campbell the fifth of Blythswood, inherited the estate of Mains by his maternal grandfather and thereafter assumed the name of Douglas.

One of the first telephone exchanges in the UK (some say the first) was at 140 Douglas Street. The Glasgow Medical Telephone Exchange opened in 1879 for the exclusive use of the medical profession. Later Douglas was immortalised in the city telephone numbers — Douglas...which became 332...

Dovehill (C/ton)

Off Gallowgate, Dovehill (Great and Little) was originally Dow Hill, about which there is a charming legend. One day St Mungo was preaching to the people on a plain making it difficult for many to see or hear him. Exercising his miraculous power, he caused the ground on which he stood to rise into a mound and then continued preaching to the satisfaction of everyone. Tradition has it that the place where this miracle happened was Dovehill and that the incident gave rise to the city's motto: 'Let Glasgow Flourish by the Preaching of the Word'.

There are three explanations for Dowhill. Dew Hill, Black Hill, from the Gaelic *dhu* and Hill of Doves derived from the small hill where 'Cushat Doos' or wild pigeons cooed and nested in the surrounding woods. Be that as it may, it was commonly known as the 'Doohills'.

Drury Street (c/c)

More contradiction here. The first meaning is theatrical in the literal sense of the word. Two youths who lived there became stagestruck through reading about London's Drury Lane Theatre. They got so carried away they had the theatre's name printed, and in a spontaneous moment pasted it to the street corner. The poster and the name stuck. Romantic, yes; true, no. The correct meaning

Old houses at the foot of Little Dovehill, Gallowgate, drawn by David Small in 1884.

is much more mundane. Drury Street was named as a compliment to Dr Drury, a prominent Glasgow physician. Its original name was West Nile Lane.

Drury Street's claim to fame comes from The Horse Shoe Bar. Incorporated from an earlier warehouse it was remodelled in 1885 by its horse-mad owner, John Scouller. Horseshoes were everywhere, even the oak and mahogany island bar was distinctively horse-shaped and until 1996 was listed in the Guinness Book of records as the longest pub bar — 104 feet 3 inches. The front and interior are largely intact and the initials JYW on the front and on a bar mirror refer to John Young Whyte, an owner in 1920s, as do the Union Jack panes transferred from his Union Café.

William Simpson's painting of the Drygate with Rottenrow in the distance.

Twenty-one Drury Street was where John Sweenie, 'a very decent Irishman' sold the best quality Irish eggs and butter and kept a sedan chair. The charge for the chair and two men was one shilling net, no tips. He thrived and retired to his native land with a modest pile. Before leaving he circularised his customers to buy lottery tickets — the prize, his sedan chair. It was not a success, everyone being afraid of drawing the lucky number.

Drygate (T/head)

This street, or what's left of it, is without doubt the oldest in Glasgow. Some people have suggested the name came about because one of the first bridges in Glasgow was built over the Molendinar Burn allowing people to cross the water without getting their feet wet. However, the official story line goes like this. In ancient times when Druids worshipped on the sacred groves of Fir Park (the Necropolis) Drygate was the only approach. The word 'dry' is Pagan and means priest. The word was brought to Scotland from Germany and applied to the pathway long before our ecclesiastical history began. Drygate therefore means the 'priest's way or road'.

In the reign of Robert III the Glasgow mint stood in Drygate. The Mercat Cross was at the junction of Drygate/Rottenrow before being removed to the foot of High Street. At the head of the street was the Duke's Lodging (the Duke of Montrose's town residence) the grandest nobleman's house in 18th century Glasgow, demolished to extend Duke Street Prison which dominated Drygate for many years. Also in the street was Glasgow's first penny school — pupils gave the master a penny each time they attended. Today, Glasgow's oldest thoroughfare is nothing more than a housing complex and a cul-de-sac.

Duke Street (T/head)

Was proposed by the Carron Company of Falkirk as a more direct route from the city through Cumbernauld to Carron. Opened in 1794 it was called Carntyne Road and renamed Duke Street because the Duke of Montrose's Lodging overlooked it. Some people say it was named after the Duke of York, Commander of the British Army at the time of the street's formation, it being the fashion to show loyalty to the throne in such a way.

A bridewell (prison) was built in Duke Street in 1798, enlarged often and rebuilt between 1875 and 1892 when a chapel and staff accommodation was added. Executions took place on an open scaffold within the prison walls. On such sombre occasions the prison bell tolled and a black flag was hoisted to the flagpole for all to see. By the end of the century it had become a female prison, the men having been removed to Barlinnie, which opened in 1872. The pleasantly landscaped Ladywell housing development replaced the forbidding, gloomy prison. However, a grim reminder of yesteryear remains — a wall inscribed with initials of murderers who were hanged in Duke Street and buried there.

Glasgow's finest remaining cotton mill, Alexander's, was built in 1848 and converted into the Great Eastern Hotel in 1909 — an imposing name for a model lodging house. Beside it is the attractive Ladywell School (1858), funded by James Alexander and built by architect John Burnet. A little further along the road stands Trinity Parish Church with its Greek façade and fluted Corinthian columns (now Kirkhaven Centre) originally built in

William Simpson's illustration of the 'Duke's Lodging', a large building that reached far behind the south side of Drygate, which it fronted. The building included two of the old Prebendal Manses connected with the Cathedral. From 1675 to 1746 it belonged to the Duke of Montrose's family. In 1849 the Prison Board acquired the property and in 1851 demolished it to make way for an extension to Duke Street Prison.

1851 as Sydney Place Presbyterian Church. Tennent's giant Wellpark Brewery (built on Well Park lands), the meat market and slaughterhouse, are also in Duke Street which has the distinction of being the longest in the UK. There was a dispute between Glasgow and London as to whether it was longer than Oxford Street. A team came up from London to find out. Glasgow won.

Dunchattan Street (T/head)

In 1777 Highlander George Macintosh built a factory on Craigs Park (east of the Cathedral) to manufacture cudbear (a vegetable dye obtained from lichen soaked in ammonia). About 2,500 gallons of urine were used each day to produce the dye. To keep the process secret he built a ten-foot-high wall around the works and on a hill in the centre of the property erected a villa named Dunchattan (home of the Macintosh). The Macintoshes are chiefs of the Clan Chattan. Here he surrounded himself with trusted Gaelic-speaking highlanders, all sworn to secrecy and mostly residing within the 17-acre enclosure. So Highland was the little community, and so isolated from the outside world, that many of its members lived and died within the walls without being able to make themselves understood in decent English. The place was called 'The Secret Work'. The Gateway and Porter's Lodge stood in Duke Street just beyond the present Dunchattan Street that took its name from the mansion. Sir John Moore, the hero of Corunna, was a clerk in the dyeworks. George's son Charles gained fame for his invention, the waterproof, a sort of smock frock of india-rubber cloth known worldwide as the 'macintosh' or' for short' 'mac'.

Dunlop Street (St/E)

This street, formed in 1772, honours Provost Colin Dunlop whose firm was one of the city's largest importers of tobacco. It weathered the revolt of the American colonies but went under in the 1793 financial crisis, 16 years after the Provost died. He was a partner in the Ropework and an original partner in the Ship Bank. Dunlop bought ground in 1748 on the south side of Westergait (Argyle Street) where he built his mansion in 1750, the second in the street and the twin of the first. When the American War of Independence began, he raised a regiment of 1,000 men for the King at the citizens' expense. For his loyalty he was offered a knighthood but declined.

The magnificent theatre on Dunlop Street's east side opened its doors in 1782. Great stars appeared there — Mrs Sarah Siddons in 1785, Paganini in 1833 and the Swedish Nightingale, Jenny Lind and Dickens in 1848. Disaster struck in 1849 when there was a false alarm of fire. In the resulting panic 65 people were trampled to death. Fourteen years later fire *did* destroy the theatre, and, although rebuilt, it had only six years of life left. The City Union Railway Company bought it in 1869 and built St Enoch Station on the site. Today, the giant glass-roofed St Enoch Centre that covers most of Dunlop Street takes its place.

In 1896 the only 'medical whisky' on the market — 'McNish's Doctor's Special' — could be bought at 92 Dunlop Street, and D

Dunlop Street's Theatre Royal. One of the railway bridges to St Enoch Station replaced it.

Sutherland's Fish, Game and Poultry establishment operated from Nos. 8-12.

Fleshers' Haugh (e/g/g)

This has a straightforward meaning: *Flesher* because the land was rented by the Incorporation of Fleshers and *Haugh* for 'Meadow'. As cattle grazed on the green, the fleshers carried on their trade there. Fleshers' Haugh used to be Provost's Haugh — reserved for Glasgow's Provosts. The city bought it from Patrick Bell in 1792 for £4,000 and the large piece of swampy ground was raised to the level of the rest of the Green around 1896 with material from railway excavations. During the improvements an intact 4th century Samian bowl was uncovered, and it now resides in the People's Palace. Charles Edward Stuart reviewed his highland army on Fleshers' Haugh in December 1745 while standing under a thorn tree thereafter known as 'Prince Charlie's Tree'. Both Rangers (1873) and Celtic (1888) football teams have their origins in the 'Haugh'. Today it is still football-orientated, with twenty pitches regularly used by amateur clubs. However, come Glasgow Fair and all the fun of the carnival takes over.

Gallowgate (C/ton)

One of Glasgow's eight original streets. And yes, it does get its name from being the way to the gallows that were around today's Barrack Street until their removal elsewhere in 1765. Gallowgate Street (1100), built on the Gallow Muir (Common) has its fair share of history, some already covered in previous pages — both Battles of the Butts, Large and Little Dovehills, the Army Barracks and the Barrows.

Just beyond Glasgow Cross is the quaintly named Schipka Pass (a battle between Russians and Turks) which used to be under cover, a sort of one-sided arcade. Now only the name is quaint. Across the road and down a bit was Glasgow's first real hotel, 'The Saracen's Head Inn', which got its name from London's famous

Old houses in Gallowgate.

Saracen's Head, named in honour of St Thomas of Canterbury whose maternal grandfather was a Saracen. Built in 1754 on the site of Little Saint Mungo's Chapel with stones from the ruins of the Bishop's Castle, it boasted an enormous ballroom and stables for 60 horses. Waiters wore powdered wigs, embroidered coats and red plush breeches, as did the two handsome porters who took in the guests' luggage from the stage coaches which all stopped at the Saracen's Head. Anyone who was anyone stayed there. The inn was demolished in 1903, but its great punch bowl, over 250 years old and slightly the worse for wear, is on view in the People's Palace.

Two of Gallowgate's old crow-stepped tenements, both built in 1771, have been renovated — No. 394, with circular stairtower leading to three floors of houses and No. 379, the ground floor housing the Heilan Jessie public house. At the Camlachie end of Gallowgate, A G Barr plc manufacture Scotland's other National Drink, 'Irn-Bru'.

Garnethill

Once known as the Summerhill, the highest hill in the city. In olden times three open air assemblies enlivened Glasgow's municipal year, the ground on which the midsummer one was held being known as 'The Summerhill'. It was also the finishing point for the perambulation of the marches ceremony that started at the Stablegreen (Bishop's Castle). In covenanting days the Highland Host camped on the Summerhill giving it a nickname 'The Hielandman's Hill'.

Dr Thomas Garnet, Professor of Natural Philosophy at Anderson's College, purchased part of Summerhill where he built his house and garden. He was closely associated with the Observatory opened on the brow of the hill in 1810 by the Glasgow Astronomical Institution. Unfortunately, because of Glasgow's industrial smoke and lack of public and government interest, it did not survive beyond mid-century. Garnethill (obviously named after Dr Garnet) developed from 1820 and was described as 'a leafy suburban quarter dotted over with detached residences'. A few survive — Nos. 120, 122, 125 and 135 Hill Street.

Although architecturally there is much of interest in Garnethill, by far the most important is the School of Art in Renfrew Street, Charles Rennie Mackintosh's masterpiece designed in 1897. Garnethill Synagogue (1881), one of the oldest in Britain, is instantly recognisable by its round arched Romanesque portal, and its unaltered interior is a marvellous reminder of times past. St Aloysius College (1883) is a Renaissance-style palazzo, and Peel Terrace (1841), one of the city's finest tenements, commemorates Sir Robert Peel who passed the Reform Bill in 1832. From his name came the nickname 'peeler' for a policeman, and from his interest in the cause of Orangeism, his Parliament colleagues referred to him as 'orange Peel'. Breadalbane Terrace (after the Earl of Breadalbane) was skilfully designed to look like individual houses instead of flats. According to an advertisement in the *Glasgow Herald* of 12 February 1869 'the properties were very desirably situated upon rising ground in Garnethill, the drainage perfect and the air salubrious'. They also had their own water supply from a private reservoir on the hill. Rose Street's art deco Film Theatre (the Cosmo Cinema which introduced European and specialised films to Glasgow's cinemagoers) sits comfortably among its older neighbours.

George Square/George Street/West George Street (m/c)

This time royalty has the honour — King George III.

George Square

Although laid out in 1781, obviously not much more was done other than mark its boundary, as it was described as 'a hollow, filled with green-water and a favourite spot for drowning cats and dogs while its banks were the slaughtering place of horses'. However, by 1804 it was pretty well finished, the buildings on the north being particularly elegant. The first picture of the square, a caricature sketch in *The Northern Looking Glass* of June 1825, shows a broken wooden paling, women washing clothes and boys vandalising its solitary statue of Sir John Moore made from brass cannons. The original intention was to have one of George III in the centre. Later, shrubbery was planted and an iron railing

George Square and muncipal buildings.

erected. The square's enclosure so incensed the public that the railings were torn down several times. For a long time it was thought the house owners had title to the square and only they could enter it with their keys. However, that was not so, and when the Prince of Wales laid the foundation stone for the Post Office (1876) the railings disappeared for good. Afterwards, flower plots and paths were laid out and seats and proper night lighting were supplied.

George Square became Glasgow's hotel centre. The Queen's, the Wellington, and the George were converted into one, and, with another storey added, became The North British Station Hotel — now the Copthorne and the only survivor of the original square. At the north-east corner is John Burnet's Merchants' House (1877) with domed tower topped by a model of a merchant ship in full sail across the world, a replica of the one that crowned the original Merchants' Steeple in the Bridgegate. Dominating the south end is William Young's City Chambers (1883) usually described as 'a free and dignified treatment of Italian Renaissance'. The interior is even more impressive — columns and staircases of granite and marble, arched ceilings and domes of Venetian mosaic. The town mansion of the Alexanders of Ballochmyle once occupied the site and it was there in 1843 that Wilhelmina Alexander, the heroine of Burns's song 'The Bonnie Lass o' Ballochmyle' died.

Twelve statues adorn George Square — Walter Scott, William Ewart, Gladstone, Robert Peel, Queen Victoria, Prince Albert, James Watt, Robert Burns, Lord Clydesdale (Colin Campbell), Thomas Campbell, Thomas Graham, James Oswald, and, as mentioned above, its first, Sir John Moore. George the III never made it

George Street

Not a long street, extending to little more than half a mile from High Street to George Square after which West George Street takes over. Well-to-do citizens favoured 'The finest street in the New Town' (1792) as a residential quarter. Sir George Burns, co-founder of the Cunard Shipping Line was born in one of its tenements, No. 118, nicknamed the 'Holy Land' because of the number of clergymen who lived there. His father was minister of the Barony Church for 72 years. No. 136, the 'Kail Kirk', belonged to a small independent sect whose members were given a plate of 'kail' between preachings each Sunday. It was in George Street that Joseph Lister's first sterilisers for his research into antiseptic surgery were made.

In 1788 the Grammar School (High School) moved to George Street, where it stayed for about forty years. When it moved out Anderson's College moved in. Incidentally, David Livingstone received his medical training there. The red stone Italianate College of Science and Technology (now part of Strathclyde University) was built on the site in 1901. Office blocks and University buildings have superseded George Street's Georgian houses and tenements.

West George Street

Stretches from George Square to Holland Street at the top of Blythswood Hill. The view down West George Street looking towards St George's Church is one of the city's finest. Originally

West George Street during the general strike in 1926 when it was used for car parking.

Camperdown Place, after the great naval victory, when Admiral Duncan routed the Dutch in 1797, it consisted of terrace houses built at the beginning of the 19th century, the earliest surviving being No. 110 (1810). Architectural gems abound, far too many to describe here so the following will have to suffice:

No. 34, Connal's Building (1899) modelled on the Ritter Inn, Heidelberg, is adorned by sculptured locomotives, ships and portrait heads of famous industrialists — James Watt, William Dixon and Connal himself among others. Charles Wilson designed No. 62 (1852) for the Royal Faculty of Procurators, the smallest, but finest example in Glasgow of the Venetian Renaissance craze of the mid 1850s. Nos. 144–146, James Sellers House (1877), the former New Club now under the banner of the Western Club, has superior sculpture by William Mossman. No. 101, William Leiper's Sun Fire & Life Assurance building (1892) won a silver medal at the Paris Exhibition of 1900. The finest surviving house in Blythswood New Town is 196 West George Street.

The street is truly commercial with representatives from practically every bank and insurance company of note.

Glassford Street (m/c)

Commemorates one of the four young men responsible for the rapid rise in Glasgow's fortunes in the 18th century, John Glassford, described as one of Europe's greatest merchants. He had 25 ships and cargoes on the seas at one time and owned extensive business enterprises in America. Indeed some of his business books are held at the Library of Congress in Washington. For his country home he had Dougalston Estate near Milngavie, and for his town house, the famous Shawfield Mansion, facing Stockwell Street, which he co-owned with Colonel McDowell of Garthland. During the American War of Independence he supported the rebels while his colleagues were on the Government's side. Sadly, he died (1783) in financial difficulties due to bad speculation and gambling, not the war. His epitaph in the old Ramshorn Churchyard is fitting: 'He who has seen the sunrise and the dawn of the tobacco trade from start to finish'. A fine oil paining of Glassford and his family hangs in the People's Palace. Great Glassford Street (1791) as it was first known, was laid out over the Shawfield Mansion's garden, the house being demolished in 1792 to complete the street to the south.

Glasgow's General Post Office was on the east side from 1840 to 1857. So dilapidated was the building when the Government bought it that the two upper floors had to be taken off, and for the next two-and-a-half years it stood roofless. It was from Glassford Street in 1855 that Glasgow's postmen — over seventy of them — were issued with uniforms for the first time; and very grand they were. Scarlet, swallow-tailed coat, blue vest, tall, black, satin hat with gold band and cockade. Strangely, they had to supply their own trousers. Maybe it was thought the splendour of the top half would dazzle so much that no-one would notice the nether regions.

Number 21, which stretched through to Virginia Street and had an entrance in both streets, was the scene of Victorian Glasgow's greatest financial disaster — the failure of the City of Glasgow Bank (1878) ruining great and small alike and paralysing the city's business. Its directors, manager and secretary were arrested,

This engraving by Joseph Swan shows a stagecoach passing Robert Adam's Trades House in Glassford Street. Note the roadworks in progress — some things never change!

charged with having fraudulently falsified the books and tried and convicted in Edinburgh's High Court.

Robert Adam's Trades' House (1794), the meeting place of the 14 Incorporated Trades of Glasgow, is in Glassford Street. The original Trades' House/Alms House in Old Kirk Street at Cathedral Square was used as a retreat for Incorporation members who had fallen on hard times. Placed in one of the windows was a box above which was carved in stone, 'Give to the puir and thou sal have treasur in Heavin'. Today's Trades' House is a benevolent society. Its façade is Adam's only surviving work in Glasgow and even that was refaced in 1927. The interior has been remodelled three times — James Sellars (1887), John Keppie (1916) and Walter Underwood (1955).

Goosedubs (S/mkt)

An intriguing name but not difficult to explain. Glasgow's first history by M'Ure refers to 'Provost Aird's Wynd reaching east from Stockwell Street to the foot of the Old Wynd'. The good provost who lived there had a flock of geese who enjoyed nothing more than disporting in the wynd's 'dubs' — Scots for a puddle or a small pond — giving rise to a nickname 'guis dubs'. When the lane was extended north to connect Stockwell Street with the Bridgegate the name had stuck and it was officially called Goosedubs Street. Railway development curtailed it dramatically. A resident of Goosedubs Street, Mrs Grant of Laggan, was the author of 'Oh where tell me where has your highland laddie gone' and another, old Janet Lindsay, was the first person in Glasgow to die of cholera in the 1832 epidemic.

Gordon Street (c/c)

Formed (1802) on ground belonging to Alexander Gordon, a gentleman of refined and artistic taste who collected rare and valuable paintings, something unheard of in Glasgow, for which his fellow mechants mocked him, as they thought it a waste of money. They were wrong. Years later fire destroyed Gordon's house along with most of the paintings whose value was assessed at £30,000 — priceless by today's standards. Because of his patronage of the arts he was called 'Alexander Picture Gordon'. He built a villa in Buchanan Street on the site long occupied by the Royal Bank of Scotland and to preserve his view to the west he bought the ground on which Gordon Street was built (1802). At first the south side only stretched to Mitchell Street and today that section is unchanged with the exception of No. 19, James Curruthers's 1931 art deco composition.

Four outstanding buildings dominate the street, the Ca'd'oro, No. 8, the Central Hotel and the Grosvenor. As the Ca'd'oro has already been dealt with we can move on to No. 8, long known as the Royal Bank Building, designed by Edinburgh's David Rhind as an Italianate banking palazzo for the Commercial Bank (1857) with fine sculptures by Handyside Ritchie — lions' heads and panels showing children stamping gold coins and printing banknotes.

The Central Hotel by Sir Rowan Anderson, a five-storey Jacobean, Italian extravaganza originally planned as the station's administration block, opened in 1885 with accommodation for

Gordon Street in the 1920s.

over four hundred and twenty guests and one hundred and seventy servants and officials.

The Grosvenor Building (1861), named from its famous restaurant, was designed as a warehouse by Alexander and George Thomson. Their eaved gallery was used as a pedestal in 1907 for J H Craigie's additional two storeys and twin baroque domes. Twice the building fell victim to fire — in 1864 but rebuilt identically, and in 1967 when Craigie's magnificent marble staircase and restaurant were destroyed and replaced by mundane offices.

One hundred years ago No. 17 was occupied by homoeopathic chemist M F Thompson, who manufactured and sold Nervetonine, said to cure indigestion, rheumatism, toothache, loss of memory, paralysis, etc — a panacea for all ills. Reid & Todd were at No. 56 and anyone who wanted a 'Wizard' tennis racket could get it at No. 64, The Argyle Rubber Co.

Hielandman's Umbrella (B/law)

Between Union and Hope Streets the magnificent Central Station viaduct makes a fair sized shop lined shelter. Many people were under the impression it got its familiar name because of the meanness of highlanders, in that when it rained they made a beeline to get under cover of the bridge, thereby saving the cost of an umbrella. Not so. The real reason for the nickname was that in the days when people left the highlands and islands to find work in Glasgow they were told before they left to go on a Sunday afternoon or evening to certain places under the 'Umbrella' where they would find other exiles gathered. Architect James Miller designed the bridge in 1906 with richly ornamented iron pilasters and tall multi-paned windows.

Howard Street (St/E)

Named after Sir John Howard the great prisoner reformer and philanthropist, it opened in 1789, mainly formed on the line of the old Ropework extending from Ropework Lane to Oswald Street. The eastern part from Maxwell Street to Stockwell occupied to a considerable extent the graveyard of the old Town's Hospital which was in Clyde Street a few yards east of St. Andrews Roman Catholic Cathedral. The boilers for Henry Bell's *Comet,* were made in David Napier's Howard Street foundry.

The street has a unique place in the history of British multiple grocery stores, particularly in relation to tea. Thomas A Bishop, founder of grocery chain Cooper & Co (1871) introduced the tea packet into Scotland. His first shop (originally tea) was in Howard Court and the company's headquarters remained in Howard Street until Fine Fare bought them out. Thomas Lipton, the hugely successful, most famous figure in the Glasgow tea and grocery trade had a large store at the corner of Howard/Jamaica Street. Another notable business began in the street, Creamola Food Products which 'tickled the world's palate in 1904'. Many will remember Creamola custard (their original product), blanc-mange, milk jellies and the children's favourite, Creamola Foam lemonade crystals.

Original early 19th-century four-storey tenements survive at Nos. 40–58, but most of the north side was swallowed up by St Enoch Station in the 1870s and the St Enoch Centre in the late 1980s.

Hutcheson Street/Hutcheson's Hall (m/c)

Both took their name from brothers George and Thomas Hutcheson who founded Hutchesons' Hospital (1639) to provide

Hutcheson's Hall, today the property of the National Trust.

shelter for several poor aged tradesmen and a school for twelve orphan boys, those named Hutcheson being given preference (the forerunner of Hutchesons' Grammar School). Begun 1641 and finished 1650, the hospital stood a little back from the Trongate with gardens running up to the Back Cow Loan (Ingram Street). It had six dormitories for the pensioners, one for the boys, two apartments for the schoolmaster, a schoolroom, sitting room, kitchen and hall. So that they might get the full benefit of their education the boys had no house duties imposed of them. Pensioners were allowed 4d a day for maintenance, a gown a year, basic foodstuffs and a leg of beef each month.

Hutcheson Street (1790) was initially formed through the hospital's gardens from Ingram Street. Later, during demolition of the hospital to complete the street, a stone from its steeple fell on a workman killing him. Some of the original, plain tenements lining both sides of the street remain.

Hutchesons' Hall (1805), built in Ingram Street to replace the old hospital, faces down Hutcheson Street and was deliberately designed by David Hamilton to look older to keep something of the atmosphere of the original. Recessed behind Corinthian columns, the principal storey is flanked by niches holding statues of George and Thomas Hutcheson carved in 1649 by James Colquhoun which came from the 17th-century hospital. Its clock faced steeple changes from square to drum to conical as it climbs. The new building was never a hospital or a school, but the home of Hutcheson's Trust which administered among other things, Hutchesons' Boys' School and Hutchesons' Girls' school whose pupils were colloquially known as 'Hutchie Bugs'. Stirling's Library was located there in the first half of the 19th century. Today, in the hands of the National Trust for Scotland it provides an elegant backdrop to an otherwise unprepossessing street.

From 1843 to 1863 The Merchants' House conducted its business from Hutcheson Street in an impressive 10 Corinthian columned building adjoining the City and County Buildings. It looked directly across Garth Street to the rival Trades House.

Ingram Street (m/c)

Forms the spine of the merchant city from Queen Street to High Street (initially only to Candleriggs the east part being Canon Row). Originally the Back Cow Loan leading to the city's grazing grounds at Cowcaddens and named in recognition of Archibald Ingram Lord Provost and Dean of Guild. An authority on finance, he did much for Glasgow and it is fitting his memory is perpetuated in a street name and in a handsome plaque hanging above the mantlepiece in the Merchants' House Directors' Room.

With so much of interest in Ingram Street (1781) it's difficult to know where to start. However, here goes. It was in the Star Inn that the Reform Association met under the leadership of Thomas Muir charged in 1764 with sedition and brought before the High Court in Edinburgh where he and others were sentenced to fourteen years transportation to Botany Bay. Also, the Inn was the starting place of the Edinburgh/Glasgow coach 'The Royal Telegraph' on 10 January 1799. William Burn's dignified Bank of Scotland building (1828) replaced the Star as the focal point up Glassford Street and is now the upmarket Italian Centre.

Robert and James Adam's Assembly Rooms, the centre of the city's social life had attractions ranging from the sublime, the composer Liszt gave two concerts, to the ridiculous, NAPOLEON BREATHING, the most wonderful anatomical figure in the world, composed of a new artificial substance, 'Sarkomos'. When the building was demolished to make way for an extension to the Post Office in 1892, at his own expense, Bailie James McLennan removed the wonderful arch forming the façade's centrepiece and had it rebuilt at the east end of London Road. Later it was removed to its present position near the Saltmarket entrance to Glasgow Green where it makes an impressive gateway and serves as a monument to Bailie McLennan's generosity.

David Hamilton's built his Union Bank (1841) on the site of the Virginia Mansion and in 1879 the addition of an elaborate frontage with statues by John Mossman to the bank created Lanarkshire House (No 91). From the side it's easy to see where the two parts meet.

Ingram Street's most fantastic building is R W Billings' 1854 gabled, turretted confection of a warehouse built for J & W Campbell & Co. When Provost James Campbell found out that the Council proposed extending the Municipal Buildings into Ingram Street he was so anxious his handsome property would not be obscured that he arranged for the front of the building to be slightly angled to the south so that anyone walking along the street would have an unrestricted view of it.

Kate Cranston chose Ingram Street (the French style building by Boucher at the west corner of Miller Street) for her first tearoom. The interior by Charles Rennie Mackintosh was moved to the Kelvingrove Art Galleries in 1971. In 1889, from No. 16, J Lizars, opticians, undertook to correct defective eyesight as far as it is possible to do so with spectacles of the highest quality — best glass spectacles 3/6d.

Engraving by Joseph Swan showing the Ramshorn Church on the right, the spire of Hutchesons' Hospital in the centre and the Cunninghame mansion which is now the Gallery of Modern Art at the end of the street.

Of Ingram Street's two most interesting buildings, Hutchesons' Hospital and the Ramshorn Kirk, the former has already been mentioned and the latter will be later.

Jamaica Street/Bridge (B/law)

Jamaica where the rum and sugar come from. Glasgow's merchants did not only make fortunes from tobacco, they made them from the lucrative West Indies trade, especially sugar and when a new thoroughfare was opened at the height of the boom it became Jamaica Street (1767). Unfortunately, for many years it remained forlorn and neglected due to the bottlework's existence at the south east corner, which poisoned the area with volumes of noxious smoke from its great cone of a chimney. When this business ceased Jamaica Street expanded into one of the busiest in the city.

When the Jamaica Bridge was built (1772) it was only 30 feet wide within the parapets. Twice it was rebuilt — by Thomas Telford in 1836 with seven arches and in 1891 when it was

This picture of Jamaica Street in 1888 shows on the left Wilson's Colosseum store and slightly further north, Gardner's famous iron building. One tramcar advertises the Daily Mail and a clothing shop at No. 54 Trongate, and the other has a destination of the Exhibition which took place that year at Kelvingrove.

redesigned with four arches but changed almost to a replica of Telford's after an outcry in Glasgow against not retaining the beautiful lines of his bridge.

A building in Jamaica Street housed the Royal Circus or 'Riding School' as it was called. There, members of the Royal Glasgow Volunteer Light Horse drilled their horses to walk, trot and gallop round the arena. The circus was turned into a place of worship, The Tabernacle of the Independents of the Congregational Union of Scotland. During its opening ceremony in 1799 an alarm was given that the galleries were giving way causing a panic resulting in many being injured.

In the mid-19th century the trysting place for highlanders living in the city was at the Broomielaw end of Jamaica Street. Dressed in their best they gathered there, particularly on Sunday evenings, to discuss family affairs and exchange reminiscences with friends. Later the venue changed to the Hielandman's Umbrella (the central station viaduct in Argyle Street).

Jamaica Street is famous for its cast iron warehouses. No. 36, known for over a century as Gardner's Iron Building (1855) is particularly important being the first to adapt the principles of the Crystal Palace's structure to commercial building. Ironfounder R McConnell patented and designed the frame and architect John Baird added the detailing of the delicate, cast-iron, arcaded façades.

Walter Wilson's Colosseum Warehouse, which opened around 1869 as a hat shop then expanded to thirty different departments, catered for a predominantly working class clientele. In contrast, gents outfitters, Paisley's, at the west Broomielaw corner, was a very high class establishment indeed, its uniforms for the services being especially outstanding. India-rubber manufacturers and waterproofers Thornton, Currie & Co, (later Currie Thomson) sold everything for a rainy day and, according to an advert of 1879, indestructible rubber toys.

James Watt Street (B/law)

Yes, obviously honours James Watt of steam engine fame. But why this street in particular, previously known as Delftfield Lane? The reason is quite simple. For several years he lived and worked in a villa there. Delftfield (named after the town of Delft in Holland) was part of the Broomielaw Croft lying between Robertson Street and Brown Street and the site of Scotland's first factory for the manufacture of delft pottery (1748) which employed James Watt in an advisory capacity. Josiah Wedgwood referred to Watt as 'some years a potter in Scotland'. It was from the Delftfield Lane house that he began his experiments into improving the steam engine.

James Watt Street (1849), has some of the handsomest surviving warehouses in Glasgow. The grandest (Nos. 44–54) is the former grain and general store built for Thomas Mann (1861) with palace front and pedimented end pavilions.

Numbers 41–45 were originally one storey plus basement designed in 1854 by John Baird with sculpture by John Mossman. However, when converted into a tobacco bond for Connal & Co around 1870 they added another storey topped by the 1854

This illustration by William Simpson shows James Watt's house in Delftfield Lane.

pediment with the 'Tobacco Warehouse' inscription and royal arms by Mossman. Baird & Thomson added further storeys in 1911.

On 18 November 1968, a warehouse occupied by an upholstery company went on fire with tragic consequences. Steel bars over the windows prevented all inside, except three, from escaping and bodies were found piled behind a padlocked fire exit. Twenty-two died. A survivor said the showroom went up like a box of fireworks and eye witnesses told of how they saw people behind the first-floor windows vainly attempting to force the iron grilles. Despite the expertise of 20 fire units, the building was a burnt-out shell.

Jocelyn Square (S/mkt)

Was once part of the old green (between Saltmarket and Jamaica Street) and became Jail Square when the Justiciary Courts and south jail were built in 1807 at the foot of Saltmarket. Prisoners were conducted from a particular cell through an underground passage to the bar, where they appeared in front of the bench without coming into contact with the spectators. Criminals condemned to death were hanged and then buried in the jail's

Seal of Bishop Jocelyn.

inner court. The last public hanging took place on 28 July 1865 — Dr Edward William Pritchard, for poisoning his wife and mother-in-law.

At the entrance to Jocelyn Square stands the City Mortuary, a red-brick building built on the burial ground of those publicly hanged. When workmen were laying its foundations and pipes they came across Pritchard's skeleton, and it was said his patent-leather boots were so perfectly preserved that they were promptly sold. Would the buyer have been as happy with his purchase if he had known whose boots they were?

In the 1920s Jail Square received a more becoming name, Jocelyn, commemorating Jocelyn, Bishop of Glasgow (1175–99). The name Jocelyn is of 'Sweet Saviour' in all the records of that earlier time and universally he was spoken of as a worthy and liberal minded prelate.

Prison Yard, where prisoners were executed and buried.

Fire destroyed the Cathedral in 1192, but fortunately it could not have happened at a better time if it had to happen at all. Jocelyn was the man to handle the calamity. Immediately he got King William the Lion (with whom he was on the best of terms) to authorise a charter to allow subscriptions to be collected to build a new Cathedral, consecrated in 1197. He also erected a tomb to St Mungo and the present crypt is called Jocelyn's Crypt.

Again using his influence with the King, Jocelyn obtained a charter in 1178, turning the city into a burgh, and in 1190 another, allowing an annual fair to be held (an eight-day holiday until the 1860s, when the present arrangement of the last fortnight in July was adopted). So it's Jocelyn we have to thank for our famous holiday. At one time the fair was held in Jail Square, its attractions — circus, freak shows, pie-shops, beer tents, merry-go-rounds — all the wonderful things our ancestors enjoyed, reaching down to the river.

Jocelyn is also remembered for his history of St Mungo, without which Glasgow would have known very little about its patron saint. The Bishop died in 1199.

John Street (m/c)

This one caused no headaches in the planning department. As so many of the council's dignitaries, including the Lord Provost, were Johns, the name was bestowed on the new street (1785) as a compliment to them, although it should really have been used in the plural form.

In 1793 a market called 'new market' was built on the north side of Cochrane/George Streets and in 1798 the flesh market on the west side of John Street was converted into Anderson's College founded 1786 by John Anderson, Professor of Oriental Languages and Natural Philosophy in the University. When the Bank of Scotland bought the building in 1827 the college was transferred to the Grammar School building in George Street which became vacant when a new school was opened in John Street.

Crossed by two magnificent arches linking the Municipal Buildings with their extension, John Street was once known as the 'sinister street' of Glasgow, it being the home of the dreaded 'rates office'. It was also the home of hero Lord Clyde (Sir Colin Campbell) who was born in No. 63 in 1792. Born Colin McLiver, he took his mother's name of Campbell when granted a commission in the army. He fought in the Sikh wars and in the Crimea, and as Commander-in-Chief in India engineered the relief of Lucknow. His statue (1868) stands in George Square not far from his birthplace.

Along the street's west side a symmetrical terrace of warehouses (1840) has been reconstructed round a courtyard — the Italian Centre. At the north east corner, No. 18, built in 1858 for the United Presbyterian Church, looks nothing like a church. It's more like an Italian palazzo, and inside, its conversion to a restaurant has obscured the wonderfully ornate ceiling.

Ladywell Street (C/dral)

Just below the slope of the Necropolis, Ladywell Street is one of the city's most ancient paths, having originally been the main route from the south east up to the Cathedral. The name originates from the Lady Well (Well of our Lady), said to have been for the use of the common people who were not allowed to use the nearby Priests' Well. Because of drainings from the Necropolis polluting the water, the well (which is in the form of an urn) was stoned up around 1820. However, it can still be seen in a niche at the street's north side. A plaque tells us it was restored in 1836, rebuilt in 1874 by the Merchants House and restored again in 1983 by Tennent Caledonian Breweries.

Ashamedly, Ladywell Street, a spot so closely connected with the origins of Glasgow and once a holy and beautiful place, is now

The thatched building to the right of Ladywell Street was the last to remain in Glasgow. At one time it was said to be where the public hangman, Calcraft, lived, giving the slope locally the name of 'Hangman's Brae'. Its outside stair had a jawbox (a sink used by all the tenants) at the top. The small single building to the left of the picture was the old ragged school, and at the extreme end of the street was the Ladywell, giving it its name.

nothing more than an empty cul-de-sac with the well at the end. However, in the days when buildings lined the street the earliest 'Ragged School' in Glasgow was on the east side. There, the Bible and Johnson's Dictionary were the main books used for instruction, and in winter each pupil had to bring a lump of coal to help warm the place. There was a Ladywell Parish Church, but that vanished years ago in the wake of the brewery.

Miller Street (m/c)

This street is narrow because of the greed of John Miller who owned a fine villa fronting Argyle Street with grounds to the back. Wishing to capitalise on rising land values, Miller decided to feu his garden into a new street as others had done very profitably. However, his surveyor recommended that the house should be demolished as it would be in the way, which suggestion Mr Miller rejected on the grounds of needless extravagance. Nevertheless, he did agree to demolish half of it and live in the part that was left. That's why the street is narrower than its neighbours.

John Miller may not have been fussy about the width of the street, but he was about its appearance. He insisted it should consist only of self-contained gentlemen's dwellings, none to be higher than two storeys and with no gable chimneys or corbie steps to face the street. His intention was to close the street at the top, as he did not want it to be a thoroughfare for carts. But when the residents applied to have it paved and lit by the council their request was refused because of the gate and wall at the north end. However, after agreement that the street would become a public highway it got its pavements and lights.

Number 7 was bought by Walter Stirling who, because of a deformity, was known as 'Humphy Watty'. When Walter died unmarried in 1791 he left his house, books and some money to establish the first free library in Scotland, Glasgow's Stirling Library. Numbers 48-56 (1863) were built on the site of Mr Stirling's old house to accommodate his bequest to the city. The library has had many moves in its lifetime but is now back in Miller Street, although not in its first home, which is next door.

Walter Stirling's House in 1791, demolished to make way for custom-built accommodation to house the collection of books he bequeathed to the city.

There is only one survivor of the original detached villas, No. 42, which, for many years, lay in a state of dilapidation minus its wings and urns. Happily, it was renovated in 1995. All the others were replaced by warehouses and factories, and No. 81 (1849) by James Salmon, is Glasgow's finest surviving textile warehouse. As with many other buildings in the Merchant City, its refined elegance has been converted into flats.

Mitchell Street (c/c)

Derived its name from a Mr Mitchell who had a distillery there — not from Stephen Mitchell, founder of the Mitchell Library, as many believed. The narrow, irregular south section, filled on the east side with the backs of Buchanan Street's shops, reflects its origin as a country lane.

At the corners of Mitchell Lane are two buildings worthy of comment. The former Glasgow Herald Building (1893), remodelled by Charles Rennie Mackintosh whilst employed by Honeyman & Keppie, with its 150-foot octagonal water tower, the full impact of which can be seen from Gordon Street, and Gordon Chambers (1903), offices, warehouses, a pub and a car showroom selling all models of Peugeots from the Baby at £160 to the Pullman at £1,000. Publican David Ross, whose original pub front remains, had Gordon Chambers built. Today shops replace the car showroom.

Molendinar Street (C/ton)

Consists now only of a signpost and railway arches turned into shops. Be that as it may, the name goes back to Glasgow's beginnings when St Mungo built his wooden church on the banks of the Molendinar Burn and it would be inexcusable not to explain its meaning.

In bygone times this once limpid streamlet rising in Hogganfield Loch flowed past the Cathedral and across the Gallowgate before joining the Clyde at a point near today's Albert Bridge. It has long been covered over and turned into a sewer. As to how it got its name, there are various accounts. Some say its origin is Latin, others Gaelic. In the latter tongue two versions are recorded — *Meall an dhuinn ard,* the stream or hill with the brown top (which is how Glasgow's early settlers would have described the present Necropolis hill) and *Muileaun,* a mill, and *Aar,* a father or abbot; *Muileaun-aar,* the Mill of the Abbot. The Latin derivation comes from the adjective *Molendinarius,* pertaining to a mill. *Molendinarius Rivus,* is the Mill Burn; and, as names are often abbreviated, *Rivus* may have been lost in usage. So once again, in the case of a puzzling name, it's a matter of choosing the one that appeals most. However, it seems that 'Miller's Burn' is quite logical, as there were mills located beside the Molendinar Burn.

In a document dated 4 February 1446/47 Bishop Cameron allowed the burgesses to erect a mill on the 'Malyndoner' Burn. This mill and its successors on the same site existed for over four centuries. At the foot of the Drygate on the Molendinar Burn was the subdean's mill, and mention was made in 1732 of a malt mill on the burn a little below the old town's mill. By 1765 the mill was grinding snuff instead of malt. Later, used for making

Molendinar Burn at Drygate drawn by David Small in the 1880s.

files, it became known as the File Mill. All the mills driven by the waters of the Molendinar Burn are long gone.

Monteith Row (g/g)

Originally a prestigious terrace of large flats built to look like individual houses which were parallel to Great Hamilton Road (London Road) and fronted Glasgow Green.

Monteith Row owes its name to one of Glasgow's most prominent citizens of the time, Henry Monteith, who was Lord Provost in 1819 when it opened. Born in Glasgow in 1765 his various business enterprises benefited the city considerably, particularly the Turkey Red industry and the manufacture of bandanna handkerchiefs. He bought the estate of Carstairs (after

Monteith Row, and beside it, the McLennan Arch where it was situated before being moved to the Saltmarket entrance to Glasgow Green.

which Carstairs Street was named) and was Member of Parliament for the Lanark Burghs in 1821.

A few years after it was built Monteith Row was in danger of losing its open outlook. When the Council planned London Road in 1824, its intention was to carry it straight along in front of the Row to what is now Bridgeton Cross. This would have eliminated the awkward turn at the western end (still there at the Old Burnt Barns pub) and made a better route for the London stagecoaches' entry into the city rather than by the Gallowgate. However, such an outcry arose from the occupants that the scheme was dropped.

Monteith Row was in a much sought after residential area and housed people of distinction — doctors, councillors, artists and wealthy merchants and manufacturers. James Templeton, founder of the world famous carpet empire, resided at No. 20, a spacious top flat with six windows overlooking the Green and with an internal stair leading to attic bedrooms. Just along the road his sons built the colourful carpet factory modelled by William Leiper on Venice's Doge's Palace. During its erection an appalling tragedy occurred. On 1 November 1888 its partially-built walls collapsed onto the adjoining weaving shed where 140 women worked. Twenty-nine were killed and 20 injured.

Opposite the Row stands a 144-feet high obelisk, Nelson's Monument (1805), the first erected to his memory in the United Kingdom, and the People's Palace and Winter Gardens, opened in 1889 to house the people's history of Glasgow.

What a shame it was thought fit to demolish Monteith Row's spacious houses with their pleasant outlook over the Green instead of refurbishing them. Only one original tenement remains, No. 14. The rest vanished in 1980 to make way for a Barratt housing development.

Morrison's Court (Argyle Street c/c)

Named after builder John Morison, who built a town house and courtyard on a vacant plot of land in Argyle Street — Morison's Court (1797). That's the correct spelling; not with two 'rr's' as it is now. Included was a coffee/eating house and from this, Sloans, Glasgow's oldest restaurant, evolved. When John built his court-yard, everyone looked upon him as being a fool who faced ruin for building so far west out of the city. He proved them wrong by making his fortune.

The coffee house became a fashionable meeting place for wealthy merchants and the courtyard was the scene of many famous cock-fighting contests — a favourite sport of the day. It was not unusual for wagers as high as 1,000 guineas to be placed on a particular fight. Twice a week the stagecoach left Morison's Court for Edinburgh, a five-hour journey. Architecturally, the Court's most important feature was a circular staircase which remains intact.

When the Arcade was built in 1828, the coffee house was pushed through into it providing access from two entrances — Morison's Court and the Arcade. It then became 'The Arcade Cafe', and when David Sloan, Manager of the Horseshoe in Drury Street, bought it in 1906 he changed it to 'Sloans Arcade Cafe', and put in hand extensive remodelling in keeping with the opulent Edwardian times.

It's worth paying a visit to Sloans. Flocked wallpaper and brass light fittings perfectly set off the rich old mahogany supplied by

Morrison's Court.

the Reid Brothers who built the Arcade, and the ornately carved ceilings in the dining room and banqueting hall are a joy to behold.

Morrison's Court has enjoyed a renaissance — freshly painted buildings, carriage lamps, and, on rare sunny days, tables and chairs set out on the ancient cobblestones. Today there is peace and quiet, no cockfights and no stage coaches clattering in and out.

Port Dundas Road (C/caddens)

Begun in 1768 the Forth & Clyde Canal was completed sea to sea in July 1790. The project cost nearly £250,000 and was partly paid for out of the estates forfeited by Jacobite sympathisers. Glasgow's chief port became Port Dundas, as a compliment to the first chairman of the Canal Company, Lawrence Dundas of Kerse, who cut the first sod when the undertaking began. The direct road to the Port (Port Dundas Road) was through Cowcaddens village

From a painting by Robert Carrick showing canal house and a fly boat about to leave. A Royal Mail van is delivering mail to the quayside.

and up the hill. A gentleman called Perter Jack built the first house in the village of Port Dundas in 1792, and the canal company built a granary, and houses for their collector and bridge-keeper.

In 1801 Lord Dundas had a steamboat constructed to replace the horses that pulled the barges along the canal. This vessel, the *Charlotte Dundas,* was the first vessel in the world to use steam propulsion commercially. However, although when launched she showed herself capable of towing heavy sloops, some proprietors objected that the wash from the paddles would erode the canal banks, and the boat was laid up in a creek adjoining the waterway where she became a wreck.

The Port Dundas Distillery, founded in 1820, now dominates the area with its conglomeration of buildings. Speirs Wharf is an upmarket flatted housing development created from the former City of Glasgow Grain Mills and Stores and the old Port Dundas Sugar Refinery.

At one time J & M P Bell's pottery was in Port Dundas, and it was the only Scottish pottery deemed good enough by the

London organisers to exhibit its goods at the Great Exhibition in 1851.

Dundas Street, the continuation of the old Cow Loan (Queen Street) leading to Cowcaddens was also named after Lord Dundas.

Provand's Lordship (T/head)

In Castle Street, facing eastward across Cathedral Square, stands a quaint old building. It's Provand's Lordship, Glasgow's oldest house, and, apart from the Cathedral, her only pre-Reformation structure. Originally the front of the house was on the west side overlooking an orchard. Still visible on a shield on the lowest corbie stone on the south gable are the armorial bearings (three acorns on a bed) of Bishop Andrew Muirhead who built it in 1471 as part of St Nicholas Hospital, providing shelter for twelve aged, poor men. (Nicholas Street off High Street, gets its name from the hospital).

Although Provand's Lordship is a strange name for a house there's nothing strange as to how it came about. After several changes of tenancy it became the official residence of the Prebendary of Barlanark and Laird of Provan. Being known as the Lord Provan and his rectory, the 'Lordship of Provan', the building popularly became 'Provand's Lordship'. A simple explanation indeed.

Two monarchs are said to have stayed in Provand's Lordship — King James IV, who held the title of Prebend of Barlanark, and his grand-daughter Mary, Queen of Scots. To perform his church duties the King visited Glasgow frequently and stayed in the handsome house belonging to his office.

Mary came to Glasgow in 1567 to visit her husband Darnley who lay sick of smallpox in his father's house. The nearby Provand's Lordship, which Mary had given to her protégé William Bailie by charter, was the only suitable lodging for her. Some of Mary's nobles plotted to kill Darnley and whether Mary was involved is one of Scottish history's most disputed points. When Mary was imprisoned in England Queen Elizabeth enquired as to why the Scottish Lords had turned against her cousin. The notorious Casket Letters, whose authenticity has always been doubted, were produced. The most damning, indicating that Mary was having

William Simpson's painting of Provand's Lordship.

an affair with Bothwell and had plotted to kill Darnley, was said to have been written by her from Provand's Lordship.

In the 18th century the building had a lean-to tagged on to it where the town executioner lived, and, as executions then took place in what is now Cathedral Square, he didn't have far to go to fulfill his gory duties. Early in the 1800s Provand's Lordship served as an alehouse which had a signboard with a painting of the Battle of The Bell o' the Brae. A drawing by William 'Crimean' Simpson from 1843 shows Provand's Lordship as a dilapidated pub. The property has also been a sweetie shop, a barber's, a greengrocer's and a soft drinks' factory.

In 1904, when demolition threatened the ancient dwelling, some public spirited citizens formed The Provand's Lordship Society with the intention of saving it for posterity. They bought the building and set about its renovation, and later, aided by grants and profits from exhibitions, converted it into today's delightful museum. Sir William Burrell gave a generous donation to provide furnishings in the style of the late 17th century. The kitchen, with heavy oak beams, stone arched fireplace and dresser lined with pewter platters, is particularly charming. There are several early Scottish oak cabinets and armchairs, a number of refectory tables and a set of ten William and Mary walnut high-backed chairs.

The windows contain some fine 16th-century stained glass. It is thanks to the endeavours of the Society that Provand's Lordship is around today.

Queen Street (c/c)

Named for Queen Charlotte, George III's consort, as it was formed on the property of Mr McColl, a zealous royalist. Being built from stone from the Black Quarry, Mr McColl's magnificent mansion at the east corner of Queen/Argyle Streets was known locally as 'McColls Black House'. Today, Next and Superdrug occupy the site. Previously known as the Cow Loan, Queen Street (1777) was a common roadway through which the town's cattle were driven up to the pastures at Cowcaddens. Cow Loan was a quagmire in wet weather and cattle often sank into it so deeply that it was extremely difficult to extricate them. It was by the Cow Loan that Cromwell entered Glasgow in 1650, having made a detour to avoid a threatened danger in the route past the Bishop's Castle. He marched down the ancient 'loan' along St Enoch's Gate (Argyle Street) and the Trongate to the Saltmarket, where he took up quarters.

Many important citizens built their mansions in the new street. Where the station stands was once the home of James Ewing who had the best rookery in the district in his grounds. He refused to have it destroyed and earned the nickname 'Craw Jamie' or 'Craw Ewing'. Kirkman Finlay, Glasgow's greatest merchant and blockade runner during the Napoleonic Wars, lived in a grand mansion near the foot of the street. The most prestigious house however, Glasgow's only surviving Tobacco Lord's mansion, was that built for John Cunninghame. In 1817 it became the property of the Royal Bank, who ten years later sold it for conversion into the Royal Exchange. Architect David Hamilton added to the front a huge portico of Corinthian columns supporting a cupola above, and to the rear a 130-feet long hall wherein the city's businessmen congregated daily. 'Craw Ewing' was the first chairman of the Royal Exchange. More than a century later the building housed the Stirling Library and is now The Gallery of

This engraving by Swan shows Queen Street after the Napoleonic Wars. On the right is the old Theatre Royal which burned to the ground in 1829 and was not rebuilt. To the left is the old Cunninghame Mansion when it was in the possession of the Royal Bank before it became the Royal Exchange.

Modern Art. The land all round the new exchange became Royal Exchange Square (from 1827).

The city's first Theatre Royal was in Queen Street, just beside the Cunninghame Mansion, but it burned to the ground in January 1829. Queen Court (1833) is the only survivor of the street's several warehouse courts. The Guild Hall (1899) at Nos. 45–46, is an iron and steel framed red-sandstone pile built as Hunter Barr's warehouse. When converted into offices the magnificent mahogany and marble entrance was sensibly retained. The National Bank and Stock Exchange formerly on the site was rebuilt at Queen's Park as Langside Hall.

Ramshorn Church (m/c)

In the middle of Ingram Street stands a square-steepled church going by the quaint name of Ramshorn. It's really St David's but has always popularly been called Ramshorn, as was its predecessor, the reason being that they were built on the Lands of Ramshorn.

Ramshorn is one of the city's oldest place-names, and much uncertainty exists regarding its origin, most explanations being legendary or fanciful. Here are three:

1. In the days of St Mungo a thief seized a ram from the Bishops' flock and cut off its head, which instantly petrified and stuck to his hand, beyond the power of man to remove. He was forced to confess his sin to St Mungo who gave him absolution and also a gift of the ram. The scene of this marvel was afterwards known as the Lands of Ramshorn.

2. It was said that the church's name is a reference to the monastery which collapsed before the Reformers got to it, just as the walls of Jericho collapsed before the ram's horn trumpets of the Israelites.

3. At rutting time the patriarchs of old brought their flocks into the low grounds to meet the rams in common for the propagation of a mixed breed. One night the demon of jealousy pervaded the rams insomuch that, neglecting the ewes, they began a furious battle and carried it on with so much rage that in the morning the shepherds found the ground strewn with the rams' horns. Hence Ramshorn.

As they pass in front of the Ramshorn Church few people realise that they are walking over graves which were in the original church's burial ground, but have been outside it since the widening of Ingram Street when the present church was built in 1824. The one belonging to the famous Foulis brothers who fostered the art of printing in Glasgow and founded the city's first Art School is acknowledged by the initials RF and AF cut on a paving-stone.

Many Glasgow worthies and great families are buried in the churchyard — David Dale, Robin Carrick, of the Old Ship Bank, the Glassfords, the Monteiths, the Walkinshaws, and, at the south-east corner of the inner graveyard wall in lair No. 5, Pierre Emile L'Angelier, the Frenchman who Madeleine Smith was accused of poisoning. The name James Fleming is on the stone. James's son John, who worked in the same office as L'Angelier, obtained his father's permission for his friend to be interred in their ground, although his name was not recorded. The churchyard

Ramshorn Church and graveyard.

still has a few of the heavy iron cages erected round the graves when the resurrectionists were busy in the 18th and 19th centuries.

The church is now used by the University of Strathclyde as a Theatre, and the Glasgow Development Agency was responsible for the cleaning up of the churchyard, which is open to the public. It's well worth a visit, as the names on the gravestones read like a 'Who's Who' of the people who constituted a large part of Glasgow's history.

Renfield Street/Renfrew Street

Both streets owe their names to the Campbells of Blythswood. Colin Campbell, who was Glasgow's Lord Provost in 1639, purchased the valuable area called Blythswood from the creditors of Sir George Elphinstone, whose dead body was seized for debt in 1634. Later, when the Campbells bought their estate near Renfrew it was called Renfield, which they changed to Blythswood, after their Glasgow property. In return for the adoption of Blythswood as the name of their estate, when they built two new streets in Glasgow they named them Renfield Street and Renfrew Street.

Renfield Street (c/c)

Architecturally very rich, although most of its finest buildings are side elevations of those fronting Gordon Street, West George Street, St Vincent Street, West Regent Street and Bath Street. However, linking these are some of interest. Numbers 13-17, the former Cranston's Picture House and Tea Rooms (1914), a tall white faience-clad façade by James Miller reconstructed inside in 1935 and again in 1990. No trace now of the Louis XVI lavish ground-floor tearoom decorated by John Ednie. The Odeon Film Centre (1934) built as the Paramount Cinema, and once memorable for its fin-mullioned entrance, brilliant neon 'night architecture' and superb Art Deco auditorium. Subdivided in *1969*, all its glamour has been lost, both inside and out. No. 121, The Pavilion Theatre, originally the Palace of Varieties (1902) — French Renaissance exterior in yellow terracotta with touches of blue and gold mosaic, Art Nouveau lettering and rich rococo decorated interior.

In the early 1900s 'Acceptable Gifts for Men and Women' could be bought at No. 6, where Reid & Todd resided, and the upmarket family outfitters Forsyth's dominated the corner of Gordon Street/Renfield Street.

Renfrew Street (G/hill)

Its claim to fame is Glasgow's School of Art, the result of a competition in 1896. The winners were Honeyman & Keppie, although the building has always been accepted worldwide as wholly the work of Charles Rennie Mackintosh. For many years revered as a pioneering work of the Modern Movement it is now appreciated as a brilliant eclectic design blending Arts and Crafts and Art Nouveau ideals. It took shape in two stages, 1897–99/1907–9, and bears all the hallmarks of Mackintosh's genius. The main doorway on Renfrew Street leads into the entrance hall with its low barrel-vaulted ceiling on either side. From the main staircase access is gained to the museum with its collection of

Renfield Street.

Mackintosh material, to the two-storey galleried library and to the Mackintosh Room, containing furniture and drawings by Mackintosh and others.

Robertson Street (B/law)

First called Madeira, it was formed on land belonging to wealthy West Indies merchant John Robertson who owned several sugar and cotton plantations. It contains one of Glasgow's architectural showpieces, the Clyde Port Authority building (from 1882) by Sir J J Burnet. The Clyde Navigation Trust rivalled the Council in power and influence and its headquarters reflected this with a spectacular corner dome and magnificent sculptures. The interior is just as splendid as the City Chambers, but more restrained.

Rottenrow (T/head)

This street comes next to Drygate in terms of age and must have been an important place in olden times, for at its eastern end, at the intersection of High Street/Drygate Street, stood the town's Cross. It was also the principal route west out of Glasgow.

There's been much dispute about the meaning of Rottenrow with no-one seeming to know exactly what the true one is. However, it definitely was not at first called Rottenrow Street, but the Ratton Raw, and it has been suggested that the original meaning of the word 'ratton' or 'rattoun' having been forgotten, it easily became altered to the unsavoury 'Rotten' of today.

The most commonly accepted meaning by historians was that it derived from the French word *routine* (usual) and *route* (way), the road being the usual way from the west to the Cathedral, hence 'routine route'. A more fanciful definition was that in the 16th and 17th centuries the word 'rattoun' was a slang word applied to women, and as it was the most attractive street in the town it would naturally have been the ladies' favourite parade — 'ladies row or walk'. Two more suggestions were, *Route du Roi* (the King's Way) and *Rath-toun-raw* (road leading to the town fortress). The prefix 'rat' is believed to have come from the Celtic *rath* (a fort or homestead) and 'raw' is the Scottish synonym for street, so it is easy to arrive at the colloquial ratounraw. However, these were

Old close in Rottenrow.

argued against on the grounds that the first was too French for the homely Scots and the second did not explain the Rottenrow of Hyde Park.

Rottenrow was a place where clerics and schoolmasters lived, and it was there that Glasgow University began in 1454. A newspaper advertisement of 1780 announced 'summer quarters to let consisting of a neat well furnished house at the west end of Rottenraw, pleasantly situated upon common gardens'. David Livingstone's first lodgings in the city were in Rottenrow, and the renowned preacher Dr Thomas Chalmers lived there.

Today as a street Rottenrow is mostly gone. There are no neat houses, but there are University buildings, albeit of the modern variety, and Glasgow's Royal Maternity Hospital (1906) a giant, gaunt, grey building with the partly blocked arcaded carriage entrance its only embellishment.

Royalty

Glasgow was very loyal to the House of Hanover, commemorating it in many of its street names.

King Street of the Sugar House and the Misses Logan's boarding school for young ladies, was attributed to George II. George Square, George Street, West George Street, Queen Street and Charlotte Street have already been explained as being named

McNair's Building, King Street. Robert McNair was born in 1703 and by industry and frugality amassed a fortune. He and his wife, a somewhat eccentric couple, had a shop in the Trongate described as having two bow windows and an exterior painted bright green. He was one of the first to introduce the blatant style of modern advertising. The King Street tenement was built for speculation. In 1783 Frazer's Dancing Hall, the principal school of etiquette, occupied one of the flats, and in a small, ill lit, back room the city's first public billiard table was kept.

in honour of George III and his Queen, who had 14 children. Their eldest son, known familiarly as the Prince Regent, later George IV, was responsible for West Regent Street. Other family members gave their names to North Frederick Street, York Street and Cambridge Street. Adelaide Place, with its great church, got its name from William IV's wife, and Kent Road (Calton) from the Duchess of Kent, Queen Victoria's mother. North Hanover Street (1787), stretching from George Square to Dobbies Loan, needs no clarification. In the heart of the merchant city, Brunswick Street honours George IV's wife Caroline, a Princess of Brunswick. She was very badly treated by the King and Glasgow felt great sympathy towards her.

Three of Glasgow's bridges carry royal names — Victoria, Albert and King George V.

St Enoch Square

St Enoch is a corruption of St Thenew, the mother of St Mungo, Glasgow's Patron Saint. Long ago there was a little chapel and graveyard dedicated to St Thenew, and it was on this site that St Enoch Square (1778) was built round a pleasant steepled church erected in 1780 by James Jaffrey. The Square had a grassy enclosure in the centre where sheep grazed and volunteers paraded. Round its railings stood sedan-chairmen ready for hire, as St Enoch Square was a kind of terminus, hiring charges being calculated from there. On the east side was the Surgeon's Hall with the Custom House's office on the west. Several handsome mansions also adorned the aristocratic quadrangle. David Hamilton's more classical building replaced Jaffrey's church in 1827, although the original steeple was retained. St Enoch church closed the vista down Buchanan Street until it was demolished in 1925.

The first major railway bridge across the River Clyde was built in the early 1870s and led into St Enoch Station (1876), the main Glasgow terminal of the Glasgow & South Western Railway. Incidentally, the station and the Post Office were the first buildings in the city to be lit by electricity (1879). The St Enoch Hotel overlooking the Square was one of Glasgow's most popular Victorian establishments, and when completed in 1880 it was

St Enoch Square in 1782 showing Jaffrey's Church and on the left the Surgeon's Hall, which, although not built by Adam, had a look of James Adam's style of architecture.

recorded as the 'most imposing structure in Glasgow'. During World War II it served as the headquarters of Naval Intelligence. Despite a public outcry the station was demolished in 1977 and the hotel two years later, the site becoming a car park until the erection of the St Enoch Centre, a massive steel and glass shopping complex.

At the corner of Argyle Street/St Enoch Square stood one of Glasgow's most famous restaurants, His Lordships' Larder, a favourite with farmers who congregated every Wednesday in the Square. There used to be a ring attached to the wall at the restaurant's side entrance for a man to tether his horse while he went inside for refreshment. For many years there was a dispute between Sloan's Arcade Café and His Lordship's Larder as to which was the oldest. However, that argument became academic when the latter was pulled down to make way for Arnott Simpson's department store which closed in 1994.

At the end of the 19th century a good bottle of whisky could be bought at Nicol Anderson's St Enoch Whisky Exchange.

Today's Square is not totally bereft of attractive and interesting buildings. The pretty, red-sandstone Jacobean styled Travel

Centre (1896), designed by James Miller as the original Underground Railway's ticket office was deliberately diminutive so as not to overshadow the church behind. Number 20, designed by James Boucher as offices for the whisky firm, William Teacher, is a four-storey Italianate building with rich carving and intricate cast-iron balconies.

St Vincent Street/St Vincent Place (comm/c)

Opened in 1804 and commemorates Admiral John Jervis's victory in the famous sea battle off Cape St Vincent (1797). St Vincent Street is the longest and straightest in the city centre and links the Merchant City westwards. It consisted of very grand terraced houses reaching Blythswood Hill, although, by the 1850s most of those closest to the centre were converted into office accommodation. The best survivor is the terrace at Nos. 206–228, retaining an intact palace-front (1825–30) and off-centre Ionic porch. Bank and insurance buildings abound in St Vincent Street/Place — Bank of Scotland, Bank of England, Clydesdale Bank, TSB, Scottish Mutual, Liverpool London & Globe, and others too many to mention. John Smith & Sons (1751), Glasgow's oldest bookshop and second oldest surviving company, operates from Nos. 49–61, a simple but elegant Renaissance palazzo (1850). In June 1994 a fire nearly destroyed the building, but fortunately, the damage was restricted to the interior.

One of Glasgow's greatest Art Nouveau architectural achievements is the 'Hatrack' (1902) by James Salmon II. Its ten floors were constructed within a single terrace house plot and its façade, mostly of glass, was held together by a red sandstone framework with fantastic detail on a minute scale. However, it is the curious rooftop cupola with projecting finials that gives the building its name. A goat or satyr's head supports the oriel with its galleon in stained glass.

The street's *pièce-de-résistance* is Alexander ('Greek') Thomson's masterpiece, the St Vincent Street Church (1859), which, built on a series of plinths and pediments, can be seen all the way from George Square. It rises like a fortress on its sloping site, culminating in a splendid Egyptian, Graeco-Roman tower. It is

Engraving by Joseph Swan of St Vincent Street around 1828.

Thomson at his most brilliant and would stand as a landmark in any city in the world. Today it is owned by the Council, who are without funds to restore or even to maintain it. Nevertheless, such is the building's importance that the Council is attempting to raise a funding package for its renovation, likely to cost around £5 million.

In the last decade of the 19th century the city's finest coach builder, John Robertson, had his premises at 412/424 St Vincent Street. The company won the Gold Medal at the Edinburgh International Exhibition in 1886 for 'Good Style, Careful Construction and High Finish'. At No. 93, G R Husband's establishment sold 'Scotch Tweed Suits for Winter' at £3, and the 'Desirable' trousers at 15/6d a pair.

Saltmarket

Used to be Waulkergate — 'the way to the colony of fullers or cloth waulkers who dwelt in a cluster of houses near the river' — and originally only stretched as far as Bridgegate where it ended in the South Port. It changed to Saltmarket in 1650 when the market that sold salt for the curing of salmon was sited there. The

Thomas Fairbairn drawing showing wooden houses at No. 77 Saltmarket, built around 1727.

thoroughfare became one of the city's most fashionable areas with 'fine lodgings' occupied by the city's merchant princes. Cromwell stayed there when he visited the city, as did the Duke of York (James VII of Scotland).

Most of medieval Saltmarket was destroyed by the Great Fire of Glasgow (1652) when more than a third of the city went up in flames. The arrival of slaughterhouses, bleachfields, the Justiciary Court and the construction of Hutcheson's Bridge in the early 19th century brought its desirability as a residential area to an end.

Today's wide and straight Saltmarket exists by courtesy of the City Improvement Trust who widened it in the early 1870s and built Glasgow's first municipal houses. These were completed in 1880 and given gables, chimneys and crowsteps to give them a look of the 17th-century buildings that had lined the street.

Glasgow's celebrated Ship Bank, its first indigenous bank, began at the corner of Bridgegate/corner of Saltmarket in 1749. The building has gone, but the Old Ship Bank pub on the same site has pictures of the original Ship Bank corner etched on its window glass. Just round the corner from the pub is Shipbank Lane, where Paddy's Market is held, so named because it was where Irish immigrants bought and sold second-hand clothing.

Around 1710 Glasgow's first Post Office opened in the Saltmarket where it remained for twenty years. At the corner of Saltmarket/ Trongate the famous Foulis brothers had an auction room which afterwards became a favourite coffee house, and in 1750 Glasgow's first haberdashery shop opened in the street. In 1763 James Watt had a shop there, and in 1788 Peter Tait, bookseller and printer of *The Glasgow Journal* which merged into *The Glasgow Herald*, conducted his business from No. 11. The space opposite the courthouse in Saltmarket was Glasgow's old showground and early theatrical quarter. There, the Glasgow Fair was held, the side-shows and attractions reaching down to the river, and there also were the City and Adelphi theatres.

Sauchiehall Street (comm/c)

It's very difficult to know where to begin when writing about Glasgow's most famous street as there's enough interesting material to fill a book never mind the few paragraphs available for this exercise.

Sauchiehall Street derived its name from being formed on a 'haugh' or meadow where 'saugh' or willow trees grew. It is a corruption of 'Sauchiehaugh' and came about by someone misinterpreting the pronunciation of 'haugh' by mistaking it for 'ha' (hall). The anglicising of Scots words led to frequent errors and occasionally actually changed the meaning. Flesher's Haugh might as well be called Flesher's Hall, which would be absurd, since 'hall' in the common acceptance of the word means a large public room.

The part of Sauchiehall Street from Buchanan Street to West Nile Street was once called Cathcart Street, the rest being a winding lane from Swan's Yett (head of Buchanan Street) to Clayslaps (Kelvingrove) until 1807, when it was widened and straightened as far as Rose Street. Thereafter villas in nice gardens

Looking east in Sauchiehall Street in the 1920s.

of an acre or so were built, followed by short terraces of self-contained houses. By 1860 the street had been widened as far as Charing Cross and connected with Dumbarton Road.

Sauchiehall Street took over from Argyle Street as the place to shop for quality goods. The leading stores were Pettigrew & Stephens and Copland and Lye. The latter's 'Caledonian House' was the earliest (1877) followed by Pettigrew's Manchester House rebuilt by John Keppie in 1897, with a dome by the young Charles Rennie Mackintosh. Both buildings were demolished in 1974 to make way for The Sauchiehall Centre; but the dome was rescued and displayed at Glasgow's Garden Festival in 1988. It's now in the Hunterian Museum. Daly's was considered a high-class store, and it was common to see chauffeur-driven limousines pulling up outside. Other well-known establishments were: Muirhead's, Henderson's, Treron's, and Watt Bros, the only survivor from the old days. Woolworth's arrived in the 1920s and Marks & Spencers in the 1930s. Only Marks remains.

Shopping is thirsty work, and for those who wanted to enjoy a cup of tea Sauchiehall Street offered the widest selection of tearooms — Skinners, M & A Browns, Craigs, Wendy's — plus those within the department stores. However, Miss Cranston's

Willow Tea-Rooms (echoing the meaning of the Street name) designed by Charles Rennie Mackintosh, were the most renowned. Today, carefully restored, the building houses a jewellery shop on the ground floor and upstairs a 'Room de-Luxe' tearoom as before. Some original features remain, the frieze in coloured glass and mirrors and the strange 'hanging rail' fireplace surrounds.

In a city famous for its cinemas and theatres, Sauchiehall Street had the best. Most of the great names of the British music hall appeared at the Empire, the largest variety hall, except for London, which started life in 1874 as the Gaiety. Not an easy house to play, English comedians nicknamed it the 'comedians' graveyard' as they were given a particularly rough reception. By 1963 the owners found it uneconomical to run and sold it to developers, as had been the fate of the Lyric (old Royalty Theatre) across the road the year before.

The Regal, La Scala, and the Gaumont were the street's three best known cinemas. The address of the Regal has had many uses including a Skating Palace, Hengler's Circus, the Waldorf Palais de Danse, and now the Cannon Film Centre. In the La Scala the restaurant was actually in the cinema and you could have a meal while watching the film. The Gaumont, with its famous fountain-court tearoom, started life as the Picture House and stood where the entrance of the Savoy Centre is today. In the 1960s *The Sound of Music* ran there for two and a half years.

Glasgow has a long tradition of keeping up with the latest dance crazes, and Sauchiehall Street provided many places to do just that — the most famous being the 'Locarno'. Grandfathers, grandmothers, fathers and mothers, all have tales to tell of their dancing days there. Jivers were not encouraged in any of the big dance halls, but the Locarno had a special place set aside for them. It became Tiffany's Disco, then the Zanzibar Nite Spot, and it's now a casino.

Art lover Archibald McLellan built the McLellan Galleries in 1855 and when he died the Council bought both the gallery and pictures. When the collection was transferred to Kelvingrove Art Galleries the building was partly reconstructed (corner dome and shopfronts created) and in 1904 Trerons moved in. New exhibition galleries and public halls with grand classical staircase were built in 1913.

Strathclyde University's Baird Hall of Residence, originally the Beresford Hotel (1938) and Glasgow's first skyscraper, was built to house visitors attending the Empire Exhibition. Its blatant Art Deco design was not appreciated by the establishment. In fact, the building with its livery of mustard and black faience with red fins, was described as 'custard and rhubarb architecture'.

John Burnet built the landmark Charing Cross Mansions (1889) a five-storey block of flats (the first time red stone was used for a building of that size) with tower, clock and wonderful French-style dormer windows. Albany Chambers, added six years later, extended the theme eastwards along Sauchiehall Street.

One or two relics from the street's original 19th-century buildings remain almost completely hidden — a late Georgian villa behind Albany Chambers, and a square two-storey dwelling with Greek Doric portico behind No. 478.

Shuttle Street (T/head)

It is hard to believe that this street, comprising of a signpost, a dilapidated building and a car park, is steeped in history. Built on the lands of Shuttlefield, it had previously been known as Greyfriars Wynd, because of its proximity to the Franciscan Monastery which stood between High Street and North Albion Street, just north of College Street. James III granted the Friars a charter in 1479 and their Monastery was destroyed at the Reformation.

In 1797 Glasgow's old meal market, built in 1696 in Shuttle Street, became a temporary prison for French soldiers who had been captured in Ireland and were *en route* to Edinburgh. At the corner of Shuttle Street and the old Grammar School Wynd was the church where David Dale acted as pastor, referred to as the 'Caun'le Kirk', having been built by Archibald Paterson, who made his money in the candle trade. The north-west and south-west corners were interesting places, the former being occupied by Greyfriars Mission School, a little thatched house demolished to build the first specially built Fire Brigade Headquarters, and

Greyfriars School, Shuttle Street, in 1829.

the latter by the old-fashioned Falstaff Inn, whose upper rooms were used by the College as chemistry laboratories. Students loved peeping into the Falstaff to see the model of a warship which hung from the rafters. On the eastern side stood St Paul's Parish Mission School, where scholars were educated for a weekly fee of three-ha'pence.

The area is one of such antiquity that digging is about to commence to establish the exact whereabouts of the Greyfriars Monastery. The University owns the site and plans to develop it for student residences and a hotel.

Spoutmouth (C/ton)

Like many other relics and places of renown in ancient Glasgow, the Spoutmouth, a small street off the Gallowgate, has been swept away. All that remains is a street sign. However, it's such an old and intriguing name that it cannot be ignored.

Glasgow Burgh Records of 1575 contained this item:

> Ye Provost and Counsale ordainis ye new common well in ye Gallowgate to be opponit daylie in ye morning and lockt at ewin and deputis Michael Pudzean to keep ye said well and key thereof.

Spoutmouth in 1861.

The well, fed from four springs, was known as the 'Four Sisters'. These springs were all directed into one spout at the 'wynd', which was given the name 'Spoutmouth'.

At Spoutmouth was a burial ground for persons who died of the plague. Three thatched houses were used as a sort of hospital, with the bodies of the dead being buried at the back of them.

Stirling Road (T/head)

Not because it was the road to Stirling, but because it was built by Wm Stirling & Sons, the city merchants and manufacturers responsible for building the Monkland Canal in 1782. It was formed due to the urgent need to provide more convenient access to the new waterway, especially from the George Square district, and to avoid the steep ascent to High Street. The title deeds referred to it as the 'Monklands Canal Road'.

The additional traffic produced a demand for building sites and soon several new streets connected Rottenrow with the new thoroughfare.

The Stirling family also laid out Stirling Street in the merchant city — now Blackfriars Street.

Stockwell Street (m/c)

One of Glasgow's eight original streets, which used to be called Fishergait, as it was the way to the salmon fishers' village. There are two stories as to how it became Stockwell Street (1345), one feasible, one fanciful. Let's start with the latter. In the days of William Wallace there was a well in Fishergait. After a skirmish there, when Wallace and his men killed many Englishmen, the bodies of the slain were thrown into the well by the victorious Scots. As they were doing so Wallace is reported to have cried 'stock it well, stock it well', from which expression the street received its name. A bit far fetched! Maybe, but there was a well in the street notable for the unsavoury taste of its water, said to be due to the bodies thrust in it. The feasible explanation is quite simple. The well was worked with a wooden stock!

The initial bridge over the Clyde was at the foot of Stockwell — the makeshift 'brig of tree'. This was followed by the first real bridge built around 1345 by Bishop Rae that went by the name of Glasgow Bridge for about five hundred years. It is interesting that in 1659 a crane with lowering tackle was erected at its north side for ducking nagging wives. The Council replaced the old bridge in 1854, and, although renaming it in honour of Queen Victoria, it was popularly called 'Stockwell Bridge', and still is.

In 1757 the Custom House was in Stockwell Street, where it remained until 1780. No. 24, Glasgow's last surviving 17th-century tenement, until 1975, when it was demolished to accommodate a car park, had an interesting history. When Bonnie Prince Charlie and his army came to Glasgow in 1745 it was there that Cameron of Lochiel lodged — the man who pleaded for Glasgow and saved it from being plundered and set on fire. The building became Garrick's Temperance Coffee House and Commercial Lodgings — and then a hotel, where it was said that Jenny Lind, the Swedish

Corner of Stockwell and Great Clyde Street in the 1840s.

Nightingale, stayed in 1847, when she gave concerts in the city. At the head of Stockwell was the stationery and music shop of MacGoune, the first man to sell pianos in Glasgow.

Glasgow's first music hall was in Stockwell Street — the Scotia, where Harry Lauder made his first professional appearance. When the music hall declined and variety took its place, the Scotia became a theatre, the Metropole, managed at the turn of the century by Arthur Jefferson, whose son Stanley occasionally helped in minor parts. Young Stanley went on to better things — as Stan Laurel, the thin doleful half of Hollywood's finest film clowns, Laurel & Hardy. Closely associated with the Metropole were Tommy Morgan, Grace Clark & Colin Murray (Mr & Mrs Glasgow), and the parents of Jimmy Logan, Jack and May Short, who played many summer seasons there. On 28 October 1961, fourteen months short of its centenary, the Metropole went on fire and was not rebuilt.

Trongate (m/c)

In ancient days the narrow lane of wooden houses between Stockwell Street and the Cross was known as St Thenew's Gate (St Enoch's street). The Tron, established by Royal Charter, was the weighing and measuring institution provided for the merchants

This picture shows the Trongate in its heyday. Horse-drawn trams advertise the Daily Mail *and the Gaiety Theatre (later the Empire), and the clocks on the Tron and Tolbooth Steeples both show the same time — 4.35 pm. Near the Tron a hanging sign of a giant boot advertises the footwear shop underneath, and further along the street a kilted soldier strides out purposefully — maybe trying to catch up on the three girls in front. Today the thoroughfare is just as busy in the evening rush hour — probably more so, but it's certainly less picturesque.*

and citizens at the market cross. Merchandise brought into the town was subject to tolls and customs collected by the Tolbooth official after weighing at the Tron. The revenue was granted to the Bishop of Glasgow by James IV in 1489, and the Tron erected at the Cross. Sometime after the street became known as Trongate — the way to the Tron.

Trongate was where Glasgow's red cloaked Tobacco Lords strutted the 'plainstanes' (pavement) in front of the arcaded Tontine Coffee Room, where the city's leading lights met to gossip and read the papers delivered daily by coach. Until the opening of the Royal Exchange The Tontine was Glasgow's commercial centre, just as Lloyds was London's. It was within the walls of the old coffee room that Glasgow's citizens first learned of Nelson's victory at Trafalgar and Wellington's at Waterloo. By the mid-19th century the elegant Tontine with stone faces adorning each arch had come down in the world by becoming Moore & Taggart's giant drapery and clothing warehouse. Gutted by fire in 1911, today's red-sandstone warehouse and office block replaced it.

In front of the Tontine stood Glasgow's first statue, William of Orange, (better known as King Billy) gifted to the city in 1753 by James McCrae, former Governor of Madras. The old cannons that form the pedestal's corner pieces were part of the armament used at the Battle of the Boyne. Since 1926 King William and his horse with the moveable tail (it had broken off and was fixed back on by a ball and socket arrangement making it sway in the breeze) have resided in Cathedral Square.

For a time the east part of the Tontine building was the Town Hall, which adjoined the Tolbooth, Glasgow's first municipal building and jail. Until 1790 the Tolbooth Steeple (1626) was surrounded with spikes, where the heads of those whose fate the authorities wished proclaimed to all in the city were stuck. By the early 1920s traffic problems were so acute around Glasgow Cross that it was proposed to clear away the Tolbooth building and steeple. The building went, which didn't really matter as it had replaced the original in 1814, but thankfully, the steeple with its imperial crown spire was saved. Although, standing in the middle of High Street like a sentinel, it's still a traffic hazard.

Trongate has another of Glasgow's historic steeples, the Tron (1636), which was all that remained after the members of the Hell Fire Club burnt the original St Mary's Church on the site to the ground in 1793. Set behind the steeple, the replacement church now houses the Tron Theatre. In the winter of 1821 gas reflectors, the invention of city pastry maker John Hart, illuminated the steeple clock dials — a United Kingdom first. The pedestrian arches were constructed in 1855. One of Glasgow's most famous sons, Sir John Moore, the hero of Corunna, was born in a tenement opposite the Tron Church.

The Council placed the first street lamps on the south-side of Trongate in 1780, as a reward for the formation of a pavement by the local shopkeepers between the Cross and Stockwell Street. In 1818 grocer James Hamilton, 128 Trongate, was the first to introduce gas lighting. A large crowd gathered to watch the phenomenon, expecting the shop to explode when the jets were lit. It didn't; and the innovation was a great success.

In Victorian times Trongate was a hotbed of vice. In less than one-sixteenth of a square mile were 200 brothels and 150 shebeens (drinking dens). In the Laigh Kirk Close alone there were 20 brothels and three shebeens.

Trongate may have lost its most famous buildings, but it still has some worthy of comment. The former Britannia Music Hall (1857), renamed the 'Panopticon' by eccentric owner, A E Pickard, was where Stan Laurel and Jack Buchanan made their débuts. This once splendid Italianate building still has the shell of the music hall and gallery in its upper floors. At the corner of Albion Street, J T Rochead, the architect who built the Wallace Monument in Stirling, designed the elaborate Scottish baronial-style Tron House for the ill-fated City of Glasgow Bank. It was the home of James Daly & Co's department store before the business moved to the more fashionable Sauchiehall Street.

The Mercat Cross was removed in 1659 and the present one, reputed to be a replica of the original, was erected in 1929. Behind it the massive Mercat Buildings (1928) stand in splendid isolation, facing west towards the Trongate.

Union Street (c/c)

At the end of the 18th century only a cart road for the conveyance of goods from Jamaica Street northwards existed where Union Street now is. The street proper began with a tenement at the east corner of Argyle Street, and as early as 1807 it was known as

Busy Union Street in the 1950s at 9.45 in the morning. Canopy of old Ca'd'Oro Restaurant is on the left and that of the Central Station on the right. The No. 32 tram went to Crookston and the 24 to Hyndland. Traffic was not one-way as it is today.

Union Place. There was no other building on that side until 1812, when the Unitarian Chapel was erected. The space between the chapel and the tenement was mostly taken up by a woodyard, which later became a horse bazaar and posting establishment. Gradually shops and residential tenements appeared, and Union Street came into being. As to how it got its name, the story goes something like this:

There were two brothers, David and James Laurie, one of whom was anxious to develop the street but had insufficient capital. He approached his brother who agreed to join forces with him financially. Building commenced, and it was said they adopted 'Union' as the street's name because it had taken their combined capital to built it. However, that sounds a bit far fetched, considering it was called Union Place before they came on the scene. It's more likely they just kept the old name, rather than invent a new one. Still, it's an interesting little anecdote.

The most outstanding building in Union street is Alexander Thomson's cast-iron framed Egyptian Halls (1871–3). Its four storeys vary in depth of relief, and the top one, of squat columns,

Indian in proportion but Egyptian in detail, forms a true eaves' gallery, pronounced the finest in Europe.

One of Glasgow's most prestigious grocers and wine merchants, J & A Ferguson, occupied No. 67 for almost a hundred years. They blended their own tea and their own brands of baking powder and cornflour were superior to any in the marketplace. Sadly, the company went the way of so many other city household names. It closed its doors in the late 1970s.

In 1886, A C Thomson at No. 113 had a Christmas message for business men: 'A girl with a knowledge of shorthand can do the work of three men by using The Caligraph Typewriter', while Wylie Lochhead Ltd at No. 96, offered to furnish shooting lodges. Shaw Walker & Co's City Ironmongery Stores occupied No. 14 in 1891. Their stock was immense and varied — grates, paraffin lamps, stoves, gasoliers and kitchen ranges, their specialities. All their goods were marked in plain figures, and the price based on the smallest possible profit. At No. 42, (A Stewart & Co) a handsome six foot oak sideboard could be bought for the princely sum of £24.10/- and an oak suite to match for £27.15/-.

The corner where the street began became famous as 'Boots Corner', once the most popular meeting place in the city. It would be impossible to count the number of people who uttered the immortal words: 'See you at Boots'. At the beginning of the 1990s a smart stone building with Art Nouveau overtones replaced the blue and white clad 1950s Boots' building.

Virginia Street (m/c)

Redolent of the trade responsible for Glasgow's rapid rise in prosperity in the 18th century, tobacco, the first street of the new town was aptly named in honour of Virginia, the American state with which the city did so much business. Provost Andrew Buchanan, who owned a large plantation there, laid out the street in 1753. When he died, his son George built the palatial Virginia Mansion which closed the view to the north. Then the house stood on the outskirts of the city, Virginia Street being the furthest west with what became Ingram Street merely a narrow drove-road leading to the country. All around were cornfields and

A mansion at the head of Virginia Street.

vegetable gardens. In 1770 another Tobacco Lord, Alexander Spiers of Elderslie, bought the mansion and later, Mrs Dalzell's well-known girls' school occupied it. In 1841, with additions by architect David Hamilton, it became the Union Bank and then with more alterations Lanarkshire House fronting Ingram Street.

The oldest building in Virginia Street is the delightful Crown Arcade (1819), a glass roofed, galleried arcade used first for tobacco and then sugar auctions. Today, it's occupied by the Virginia Antique Galleries. No. 53, Virginia Buildings (1817), replaced the mansion owned by tobacco merchant John Bowman — the best of the second-generation architecture surviving in the street. No. 52 at the corner of Wilson Street, the Courtyard Hotel, has a turnpike stair in the rear court, and No. 42, a small Italian palazzo, designed in 1867 by William Leiper and R G Melvin for the Glasgow Gas Company has been incorporated into Marks & Spencer's store which stretches back from Argyle Street.

In its early days Virginia Street was a great banking centre and has the distinction of being one of Britain's oldest banking sites.

It was there that the old Thistle Bank started in 1765, and there the City of Glasgow Bank, which failed in 1878 due to imprudent and illegal activity by the directors, had premises stretching through to Glassford Street. Some of the ruined depositors were said to have gone made mad, and one white-haired old man was seen prowling round Virginia Street with a loaded rifle ready to shoot at any bank director he came across.

Robert Burns bought fifteen yards of black silk for Jean Armour's wedding dress at a cost of £4.6s.3d from silk merchant Robert McIndoe in Virginia Street.

Washington Street (B/law)

Stands on lands once the subject of eighteen years' litigation between the Reid family and a descendant of a former owner who had surrendered them for a loan under what is known as 'Terms of Wadset' — by which the lands are absolutely conveyed to and enjoyed by the lender, the borrower paying no interest on the loan. If, however, the loan is redeemed within a specified time the borrower has no worries, but if not, the lands become absolutely and irredeemably the property of the lender. The legal marathon ended when a member of the Reid family bought off the claimant for £1,000. When the Clyde Trust offered to buy the land to build a dock, Miss Mary Reid was the owner. She asked for £10,000 which was laughed at. However, a year later they offered her £8,000. She refused and opened a street (1815) the feus realising her £30,000. Being an ardent pro-American and republican in politics, Miss Reid named her street, consisting of warehouses, flour and grain mills, after the first president of the United States — George Washington.

Watson Street (m/c)

Looking at this short street, connecting Bell Street with the Gallowgate, nothing suggests its tragic history.

It was named after James Watson, Lord Provost from 1871–74 and Glasgow's first stockbroker. Sir James, as he became, established model lodging houses in the city, one being at the corner of Watson Street, which is where part of its tragic past

Watson Street fire.

comes in. On 19 November 1905, shortly before six in the morning, the building, a converted warehouse, went on fire, and, although the fire brigade was at the scene within minutes of the alarm, the fire spread rapidly, trapping many of those on the floor where it started. In all, 39 men died and 24 were injured. *The Scotsman* editorial next day criticised the establishment's operation:

> The absence of adequate precautions against such a catastrophe, the rapid spread of the fire because of the wooden cubicles and the fact that means of escape or even access to air from the uppermost storey was only obtained after a cripple's crutch had been used to break a way through the windows.

Tragedy number two, or really number one, as it happened 21 years before the lodging house fire, was when, on 1 November 1884, a false alarm of fire was raised in the Star Variety Theatre. In the general panic and stampede to reach the exits 14 people were trampled to death and 18 injured. However, some good came out of the tragedy. The authorities introduced stringent bye-laws to prevent similar occurrences in places of public entertainment. Nevertheless, in 1952, the Queen's Theatre, as it had been renamed, *did* burn down, fortunately with no loss of life.

West Nile Street (c/c)

Glasgow was very patriotic, often naming its streets after famous generals, admirals, or battles. West Nile Street (1808) commemorates the Battle of the Nile at Aboukir Bay, near Alexandria, where, on 1 August 1798, Nelson had a great victory over the French.

Although there are some survivors of the original street — plain, classical buildings with architraved windows and, at Nos. 106–8, the former Victoria Baths (1837), most of its buildings are post-war office blocks.

Underneath West Nile Street runs a sewer, once the clear St Enoch's Burn, abounding in trout, which flowed west from the Cathedral and emptied into the Clyde. In 1837 at No. 131, Thomas Templeton sold 'real Glenlivet whisky as well as port and sherry wines and Wm Younger's Superior xxx ale'. At No. 54 Monsieur Serlorio taught dancing and etiquette over the winter months,

Fire in West Nile Street at the old Royal Restaurant.

when he returned from his annual summer visit to Paris. A familiar sight in West Nile Street until World War II was the line of trace horses waiting to help horse-drawn lorries up the steep incline to the north. Owned by Wordie & Co, the Clydesdales won many prizes at shows.

Wilson Street (m/c)

If Ingram Street is the spine of the Merchant City, Wilson Street (1793) is its heart. Named in honour of George Wilson, the founder of Wilson's Charity School that stood at the north-east corner, architect Robert Smith designed it as a continuation of Bell Street. However, his plan was thwarted as he failed to purchase the ancient mansion on the west of Candleriggs belonging to Dr Scruton's writing school. Built on garden ground, the street's buildings were all to a uniform plan disturbed by the erection of the massive, but graceful, neo-Greek City & County Buildings (1844), housing side-by-side for 30 years the municipal authorities and the Sheriffs of Lanarkshire. After the construction of the City Chambers in George Square it became a Sheriff Court.

A peculiarity of Wilson Street's buildings was that immediately behind each section were entries from one street to another known as 'Through Gang' closes, so convenient to midnight prowlers that under police regulations their iron gates were kept locked at night. From its central position and absence of any carriage traffic, the street was the stand for common carters whose services were available to the public. Their position was well marked by the remains of horses' food scattered on the road.

Today's street consists mainly of 1930s warehouses, most successfully converted into upmarket flats.